14.95

D1562100

STEPPING
OUT
WITHIN

STEPPING OUT WITHIN

*The Enneagram
as a Guide to
Relationships and Transformation*

ROBERT W. OLSON, Ph.D.

AWAKENED PRESS • SAN JUAN CAPISTRANO, CA

ISBN: 0-9634860-0-4

Library of Congress Catalog Card Number: 92-97237

Awakened Press
31921 Camino Capistrano, Suite 319
San Juan Capistrano, California 92675

Design and Typesetting by PARAGON GRAPHICS
Cover and Graphics by PARAGON GRAPHICS Newport Beach, CA
Author's Photo by Images by Dwayne
Printing by KNI, Anaheim, California

ACKNOWLEDGEMENTS

I gratefully acknowledge the assistance which I received from special people who helped me complete this book. In particular, I thank Gloria Davenport, Jay Gale, Bill Heffernen, Ron Jue, Shirley McCorkle, Sanjen and Yishana Miedzinski, Lawnee Olson, Robert D. Olson, Helen Palmer, Father Joe Scerbo, Mark Waltman, Dan Schiele and Don Zimbalist for their very helpful input. I thank my college students, workshop participants and clients for their patience and feedback.

I am thankful to Eli Jaxon Bear for introducing me to the concept of the Enneagram. The ground breaking research of Oscar Ichazo and Claudio Naranjo laid the foundation for my theoretical understanding of the Enneagram. Helen Palmer's extensive and thorough research on personality styles as they relate to the Enneagram is fundamentally important to this book. Other notable teachers and researchers who contributed substantially to my understanding of the Enneagram include Mary Beesing, Margaret Keyes, Patrick O'Leary and Don Riso.

I thank A.H. Almaas for helping me begin to integrate the process of transformation into my life, his extensive research on essence, and for his feedback on my use of the term "essence" in Part Three of this book. The foundation for my understanding of essence is based on the theoretical work of A.H. Almaas.

I thank Lorna Galbraith, whose intelligence, encouragement and compassion helped me clarify, refine and focus my writing. I thank Shiela Carlisle for her caring and skilled editing. I thank Scott Hudson for his creative and artistic design and layout of this book. And, most of all, I thank my wife Vawnee, whose love, nurturing and heartfelt feedback helped this book become more of an expression of my essence rather than simply an expression of collected facts and information.

CONTENTS

INTRODUCTION

MOTIVATION AND BACKGROUND FOR WRITING THIS BOOK

"Why do I do the things I do? Am I on the right path in life? Sometimes I wonder where life is leading me. What is life really about? What does life have to offer? Is there a better life in this world for me?"

"Sometimes, all of life confuses me. Sometimes I crave to feel and know true love, happiness and peace. How do I go about getting what I desire in life? What do I really want in life? Who is the right person for me?"

More and more, people are asking questions about who they really are. The search for self-understanding and a deeper, more fulfilling life is becoming more widespread as our society matures. As we become more psychologically sophisticated and spiritually attuned, we become aware of how much more there can be to life. Although we may already be experiencing some happiness and fulfillment, in our hearts we know we could have more.

This book is for those who seek to see their lives more clearly and live them more fully. It is for those who are ready to open themselves to self-discovery and so improve the quality of their lives, relationships and careers.

You *can* live a more fulfilled, happy and productive life. But remember that the task of using your innate capacities to reach self-understanding and growth is not easy. It is a process that often requires us to change our view of ourselves, our judgments about others and our illusions about life. Because we are frequently exposed to psychology in school, therapy, books and the movies, we expect to find penetrating answers that apply to our own specific motivations and needs. It is also for those who have a deep yearning to attain their personal potential.

For these reasons, I began to share with my clients and students the Enneagram, a map for self-understanding and inner-transformation that is estimated to be from two to three thousand years old. It was introduced to Western culture early in the twentieth century by the Russian adventurer and philosopher George Gurdjieff, who discovered the Enneagram when he was studying in Central Asia. More recently Oscar Ichazo, a philosopher and seeker, and Claudio Naranjo, a psychiatrist, have refined and expanded the fundamental concepts of the Enneagram.

The perennial wisdom of the Enneagram has stood the test of time. With its nine-point geometric shape surrounded by a circle representing humankind, the Enneagram is a detailed, sophisticated and remarkably accurate representation of nine principal personality types. It also represents combinations of the nine types which clarify the important aspects of all personalities. It describes the central underlying motivation of each type and delineates how each personality type responds to stress and relaxation. The Enneagram system describes what each personality type must do in order to grow, and what each person can expect to experience as they travel the path of inner transformation.

While sharing the Enneagram with others I discovered that they responded to this information as enthusiastically as I did when I first learned it. Feeling the power of the Enneagram and how it could help them understand other people as well as transform their own lives, they wanted to learn more and more and more. My own excitement about the Enneagram, combined with that of my students, is one of the reasons why I wrote this book. It is designed for anyone interested in human understanding, growth and development.

Many books have been written about Enneagram personality types and many books refer to the concept of essence. This book integrates these two important concepts with precision, ease and clarity. In this book for the first time a detailed description of the connection between personality types, personality development and specific aspects of essence is introduced.

For the beginner this book is designed to be an easy to understand, clear and thorough introduction to personality types, essence and transformation. For the advanced reader it is designed to help them integrate and crystallize their understanding of the various components of self-discovery and personal transformation such as the psychodynamics of personalities, personality types, personality development, levels of psychological health, defense mechanisms, essence, searching for the truth, emotions, placement of attention, presence, personal transformation, psychotherapy and interpersonal relationships.

This book combines the ancient and, until recently, unrevealed wisdom of the Enneagram with the latest in psychodynamic psychology. Reading this book will help you to identify your primary personality type and to develop greater clarity and insight into yourself.

Helping you to achieve your personal potential and understand the self-transformation process are the primary goals of this book. Identifying your personality type and the types of others are also extremely important features of this book. Identifying your own personality type will facilitate your personal growth. Identifying the personality types of others is a key to helping you communicate with and relate to family members, friends and acquaintances more effectively.

Improved clarity about your personality type and that of those around you can also be extremely beneficial in your profession. For example, psychotherapists can crystallize their understanding of their clients and accelerate the client's progress. Teachers can relate to students, administrators and parents more effectively. Business leaders can improve employee motivation; in turn, employees can understand their bosses better. Personnel directors can hire and organize people with greater effectiveness. The transformation process guided by the Enneagram can lead to improved communication and relationships at all levels, in the workplace as well as in your personal life.

How you use the Enneagram depends on you. If you are willing to immerse yourself in this book and apply what you read to your life, your discoveries and growth will be very rewarding.

The ancient wisdom of the Enneagram complements and harmonizes with the most recent discoveries in psychology.

Recent theories in psychology, such as Object Relations theory, are utilized in this book to provide a modern understanding of the ancient Enneagram. "Essence," that which is most true and real inside of you, is introduced because releasing your essence accelerates your psychological growth and leads to transformation. When essence is released and developed you become a mature and individuated person. You are freed from your identification with your childhood conditioning and traumas. You make choices based on a clear understanding of reality, and your life becomes a joyful and meaningful expression of your inner potential.

But before you become familiar with the Enneagram map, let's explore how you got to where you are now in life. As children, we develop beliefs about life which fit with the world in which we live. These beliefs are based on how we were treated as a child and on the perceived motivations of our parents and others around us. These beliefs about life are the foundation for how we love, work and play. They determine what makes us happy and what makes us sad and our personal level of happiness and sadness. We think that the world which we perceive is the real world and the only world which exists.

Early in childhood these primary beliefs are unconsciously converted into a central motivation called our "compelling desire," which is the underlying foundation for our personality. And this is the personality which is fixated and forms a shell around our essence. We rely on this shell to keep us safe and get our needs met.

But our fixated personality shell was formed when we were children and is basically unchanging. It is based on the beliefs of our parents, who learned their beliefs from their parents, etc. etc. Formed in the environment in which we lived when we were children, it is a personality which is unique to us. It is fixated and outdated. It simply doesn't apply to the changing world and society in which we exist as adults.

No wonder we have frustration in our lives, and don't know what we really want. No wonder we often settle for jobs and relationships which quickly become only mildly rewarding and for some, painful and meaningless. A life of celebration seems unrealistic - maybe for someone else, but not for us.

Almost all of us experience a nagging feeling that life *can* be more fulfilling and joyous. And most of us do try to improve ourselves and our lives. However, the ways we try to improve are based on beliefs that are no longer appropriate. Our compelling desire, which formed the basis for our personality, was developed early in childhood and no longer functions effectively in an adult world.

People usually see just one central solution for their problems, a solution based on their underlying, compelling desire. For example, Controlling personalities believe that gaining more control over themselves and others will lead to happiness. This fixed, compelling desire is the basis of their personality and dominates how they attempt to grow. But being in control only temporarily satisfies their need to feel safer and less vulnerable in life. What's worse they're stuck on one track – they aren't aware that they can grow and more fully enjoy life if they develop a more flexible and creative approach. Instead, they rely on their fixed compelling desire to control, resulting in a stagnating life and making their efforts to grow very difficult. Controlling others doesn't lead to sustained happiness.

If you want to make your life more rewarding and happy, a true and natural celebration, you must become keenly aware that your personality is really a shell and that your essential, celebrative self is restricted by this shell. So, to move from self-improvement to self-transformation, you will need to gain more access to and identify more with your essence in order to emerge from the constraints of your personality shell. This process is what I call "stepping out from within."

What is your compelling desire? What is the basis of your hope for a more rewarding life? Is it being good? Achieving? Controlling? Pleasing? Avoiding conflict? These are some of the underlying compelling desires which determine the course of peoples' lives. So, to begin the path toward a life of moment to moment celebration, the first step is to determine your compelling desire, the central underlying motivation for your life. Identifying your compelling desire is the first step in locating yourself on the Enneagram map.

As your self-transformation progresses, the healthy aspects of each of the nine personality types will become more integrated into your life. And those aspects of yourself which may be needed to face any situation in life will effortlessly and spontaneously arise when you need them. Essential aspects of yourself, such as strength, commitment, love and joy, will arise automatically when needed and when appropriate.

In order to assist you on your journey, this book is divided into three parts. Although Part One is brief, it is designed to lead you to a "burst" in your understanding of yourself and your childhood. A self-test facilitates identification of your primary personality type. The new insights are likely to occur quickly and are exciting!

Part Two provides more depth. It expands your newly developed insights to include insights into important relationships, provides additional understanding of how your compelling desire was developed in childhood, and helps you integrate new understandings and awareness into your life. Growth which occurs using the material in Part Two is slower and requires more patience. However, it is deeper, richer, and more lasting.

Part Three helps you shift your attention from the external world to your inner world, from knowledge to wisdom, and from the future and past to the present moment. The twelve levels of the transformation process are outlined, and the current level of development of your personality is clarified. At this point in your journey to personal potential, the process of transformation involves a shift in your focus from your personality to your essence. Discovering the truth about yourself and others becomes your most important goal. Now you learn to rely less on your compelling desire so that your fixated personality shell softens and your essence can be released.

The material in Part Three is the foundation for the lifelong process of transformation. Because this part of the journey is so personal and deep, it is more similar to spiritual growth than personality improvement. It is a taste of what advanced teachers of the transformation process teach.

As you progress further along your journey, you will step

out into the world supported by your essence. Instead of reacting to the world, you will assert yourself in the world. Your essence will begin to permeate your personality. You will experience love, joy, meaning and compassion, free from the control of your compelling desire. You will awaken the energy and strength necessary to continue the transformation process.

Deep within all of us is a longing to be free, to love, and to celebrate life. The process of transformation is lifelong and often difficult. But those who travel even a short way are grateful for the improvement in their life. They are able to celebrate life more fully. May your life be a true celebration!

PART 1

INITIAL SELF-UNDERSTANDING

PART ONE
INITIAL SELF-UNDERSTANDING

L oving yourself and others increases when you grow in knowledge of the truth about yourself and the human condition. Part One is a brief yet potent introduction to finding and understanding your unique personality. You will be pleasantly surprised at how quickly you will come to know yourself. The self-test and summary of the nine principal personality types will provide you with immediate insights into yourself, your loved ones, your boss and your employees.

CHAPTER
1

HOW I GOT TO BE ME

> *"Most people live... in a very restricted circle of their*
> *potential being. They make use of a very small portion of their*
> *potential consciousness, and of their soul's resources in*
> *general."*
>
> *- William James*

A scorpion approached a frog, asking the frog to give him a ride across the river. The frog protested, saying "You would certainly sting me and kill me during the journey." But the scorpion pleaded, "I must get to the other side to see my beloved wife and children. Besides, if I kill you while we are in the river, we would both drown and die." The frog gave in. They were somewhere near the middle of the river when the scorpion stung the frog. As they both were sinking to their certain deaths, the frog asked the scorpion, "Why did you sting me?" The scorpion replied, "That is what scorpions do. I couldn't help it!"

It often seems as if we're like the scorpion in this ancient parable. We're locked in fixated and sometimes self-destructive personality patterns which, as William James said, are but a very restricted portion of our potential being. Most of us aren't aware of the nature of our specific personality, what its strengths and

5

weaknesses are, where it came from, or how to change it.

After you read this chapter you will have a better understanding of how you developed your personality and the nature of your particular personality. Unlike the scorpion, whose nature is genetically determined, very restricted and can't change significantly, your personality is only a shell which can be improved dramatically. Buried inside this fixated personality shell is your deepest self, your essence.

This chapter will also introduce you to what essence is and how it got buried by your personality. It will help you begin to realize how much more there is to you, how much more to love and share with others. Later chapters will focus on achieving a deeper understanding of yourself and your relationships, and on learning how to grow and transform.

When a newborn baby's umbilical cord is cut, the baby is physically separated from its mother. However, according to Object Relations psychology, the baby remains psychologically connected for another five months. During these five months the mother and child are psychologically one. What the mother feels the child feels - and - vice versa.

Toward the end of this five-month period, the infant experiences an inner urge to begin separating from mother. And the strength to separate begins to emerge from its essence. This is the beginning of its journey to become a separate, unique individual.

At this stage of life the emerging self of the infant is fragile. It needs the support and nurturance of its environment. Trauma, conflict or painful physical or emotional environments can interfere with the emergence of the self's essential capacities. Key essential aspects of its nature which existed at birth are attempting to emerge, such as strength, value and joy, are blocked and repressed when they are not supported by the environment. When blockage of essence occurs the infant experiences emotional pain and feels an inner deficiency in the blocked area.

How is it possible for a baby to tolerate this inner pain and also become separate from mother when something as important as its inner strength is blocked? It does this by internally deadening the pain. The infant seeks compensation for the lack of its own strength by searching for the strength it needs from outside sources such as mother or some other primary caregiver.

For example, one way to compensate for this blocked inner strength is to remain dependent on and please mother. This strategy of pleasing insures that the continued support from mother can be counted on and will replace the infant's own blocked inner strength.

This pleasing personality becomes permanent by the age of about three, according to the psychological theory called Object Relations. It now becomes a shell protecting the essence of the child. The child's personality is fixated around pleasing for the rest of its life. This person will please in order to gain the support and strength of others. As you will see in more detail later, the child's personality has become fixated as a Type Two personality, or Pleaser, on the Enneagram.

The Type Two person goes through life pleasing and *believing* that this is who they are, and that pleasing is what life is all about. Pleasing to avoid abandonment are the motives which underlie most of this person's behavior. It is their way of coping with inner pain, deficiency, and lack of inner strength. But this personality is not who the person really is! It is their exterior shell which is called the personality. It is who they "think" they are.

This fixated personality shell develops in childhood and is solidified by years of parental conditioning. This person pleased and got support, pleased and got strokes, pleased and felt wanted. If they didn't please they were ignored, scolded or punished.

So what is wrong with pleasing, you ask? Nothing! But when pleasing is virtually the only way you know how to relate to others it has many drawbacks. It makes you dependent on others. Your feelings of strength come from how well you learned to please others. Your own needs are forgotten. Because you are dependent on others for strength, you live in fear of abandonment. It's difficult for you to function in the world on your own. And to compensate for your missing strength, you need people in your life who are strong and who won't abandon you.

Like the scorpion, Pleasers often do things which they regret later. Some of the people they please aren't appreciative and may treat them like doormats. They often feel like victims but, like the scorpion, they can't seem to stop their self-destructive, fixated behavior. Pleasers repress their anger while always trying to be "sweet" and, as a result, under stress they become angry and will often verbally attack others.

The gifts which Pleasers bring to relationships and the world community are their capacities to be compassionate and loving. After all, they've practiced being compassionate and loving all their lives! They are experts at perceiving someone else's need for love and kindness and they reach out in a compassionate way to help others feel loved.

As far as personal growth is concerned, the key words in the previous paragraph are "perceive someone *else's* needs," "reach *out*" and, "help *others*." Pleasers become outer or "other" directed. They are extremely deficient at perceiving *themselves*, understanding *themselves*, and giving compassionate help to *themselves*. But in the process of loving others, they experience a twofold loss. They've lost their capacity to know their own inner needs, and they've substituted giving love for directly experiencing and enjoying love. They deny their own inner capacity for self-love.

If Pleasers become aware of their predicament and begin to understand the need for self-growth, they become more able to directly experience their inner loving nature, less dependent on others, and less afraid of abandonment. And they develop the capacity to share their loving nature with others, with no need or expectation of anything in return. They begin to develop their potential for a whole and fulfilling life.

The personality development process for the Pleaser personality we've just discussed is used as an example. The same process applies to the personality development of each of us to different degrees and in different ways. Every one of us, even though we are usually not aware of it, develops a personality to compensate for blocked aspects of our essence. We become fixed in behavior patterns which are sometimes rewarding and at other times self-destructive.

The nine principal fixed personalities which develop in early childhood are described on the Enneagram as:

Type One	**The Perfectionist**
Type Two	**The Pleaser**
Type Three	**The Achiever**
Type Four	**The Artist**
Type Five	**The Thinker**
Type Six	**The Loyal-Skeptic**
Type Seven	**The Optimist**
Type Eight	**The Controller**
Type Nine	**The Peacemaker**

Taking the self-test in the next chapter is the first step in discovering your unique personality type.

All human beings want to feel self-worth. We want to love and be loved. However, most people don't know how. Like the scorpion, we are also stuck. We became stuck when our essence was blocked and our fixated personality shell was formed from beliefs we developed in childhood. To get what we want in life as adults, these childlike beliefs need to be reexamined. Our fixated personality shell needs to be softened. We need to see things as they are now.

As our fixated personality shell softens, our essence begins to emerge. Essence is that which is most true, real and precious. It is extremely difficult to describe yet when you experience it directly you recognize it. Because when you experience it, you feel like you have come home, you experience fullness of being and you feel present in the moment.

Even though your fixated personality blocks essence, it also is a distorted, muffled expression of essence. As you understand your personality more and progress along the path of transformation further, you will experience essence more directly in its various aspects such as truth, clarity, love, peace, compassion and courage. As your journey progresses you will also make greater contact with your essential self – your true self.

At deeper levels of contact with essence, you become very

clear about who you really are. You realize that your essential nature is what is most precious about you. Yet you have difficulty describing yourself because you are not fixated and contracted like you were when access to essence was blocked by your fixated personality shell. You are free and spacious. In a way, you don't feel like you exist at all and yet you experience a profound sense of well being. You seem to change moment to moment and yet feel that who you are never changes. Therefore, to describe yourself when you have progressed far along the path of transformation, you must revert to expressions which, for those who haven't made significant contact with their essential nature, are difficult to understand such as fullness of being and presence.

The content of this book grew out of decades of my own self-growth through research into the transformation process. It contains practical information which will help you become more aware about what aspects of your essence were blocked, how you have compensated for your blocks, how your fixated personality shell developed and how to replace your child-based reactions with adult-based decisions so you can live a full and rich life as a whole, effective and loving person. You can't love yourself fully if you don't even know what's inside your shell. And you can't love others if you don't know and love yourself. Love is the basis for a life of celebration.

CHAPTER

2

DETERMINING YOUR PERSONALITY TYPE

"How little do we know that which we are! How less that, we may be!"

- Byron

T he personality test which follows is very helpful in determining your Enneagram Type. **HOWEVER, SOME PEOPLE WILL INCORRECTLY IDENTIFY THEIR ENNEAGRAM NUMBER BECAUSE IT IS OFTEN DIFFICULT FOR US TO BE AWARE OF OUR UNDERLYING MOTIVES.**

The test results can **HELP** us to eventually discover our primary personality type. **USE THE TEST RESULTS AS A BEGINNING POINT IN YOUR EFFORTS TO IDENTIFY YOUR NUMBER, RATHER THAN AS AN END POINT.** As you read on in this book you will attain a clearer knowledge of your personality type.

Allow about twenty minutes to complete the test. As with all tests of this nature, respond spontaneously using the first rating which enters your mind, rather than trying too hard to make a careful choice. Place your scores for the test beside each question and then transfer your scores to the test results page provided at the end of the test.

THE OLSON ENNEAGRAM PERSONALITY TEST

The **OLSON ENNEAGRAM PERSONALITY TEST** takes about twenty minutes and is designed to help you discover your primary Enneagram type. Record your scores in the space provided beside each question, then transfer them to the test results page at the end of the test to determine your personality type.

4 *Strongly Agree,* 3 *Agree,* 2 *Disagree* 1 *Strongly Disagree*

_____ 1. I frequently think about how to do things better, and I am very self critical.

_____ 2 Love is the most important thing in life.

_____ 3. When I am working hard and accomplishing a lot, I feel best about myself. I love to work.

_____ 4. I am so sensitive to the feelings of other people that sometimes it seems like I feel their feelings in my body.

_____ 5. I pride myself in being an expert in one or more very specialized areas of knowledge.

_____ 6. It is very important for me to be loyal to other people and organizations to which I belong.

_____ 7. People should have fun and enjoy life because things will work out for the best.

_____ 8. I am lustful and willing to fight for, and go for what I want.

_____ 9. I rarely discuss my personal life with others because it is private, and they probably aren't interested in it anyway.

_____ 10. I feel people should try their hardest to be the right kind of person.

_____ 11. I spend a lot of time helping others, and I like to make them feel my love for them.

_____ 12. I want to be recognized and admired as successful at whatever I do.

_____ 13. I often have private thoughts that I am elite and creative, but at other times I feel defective and inferior.

_____ 14. I am an observer more than a participant in social activities.

_____ 15. I am uncertain and worry about what other people think of me and what they expect from me.

_____ 16. I like to be with light-hearted and playful people and I get very upset with people who interfere with my plans for fun.

_____ 17. I don't publicly show any weaknesses, and I dislike weak people.

_____ 18. It is important for me to understand, respect, and support other people's needs even though I readily give in to other's needs.

_____ 19. I can make a strong defense of my viewpoint in an argument by planning my responses well in advance.

_____ 20. People feel accepted around me and they are surprised at how easy it is to reveal very personal thoughts and feelings to me.

_____ 21. People are amazed at how much work I get done, and how scheduled my work life is.

_____ 22. I like to be mysterious and different from other people.

_____ 23. I must have my privacy, and I need a special place set aside to be by myself and think.

_____ 24. No matter how carefully I think about a decision which I need to make, I worry about how people will react.

_____ 25. People find me uplifting and fun to be with. I enjoy cheering people up.

_____ 26. I enjoy being powerful and need to be in control.

_____ 27. I rarely get angry, and I am uncomfortable when other people openly display anger.

_____ 28. I am proud of my high ideals, and often find myself re-doing tasks to do them as well as I can.

_____ 29. It is important for me to feel loved and needed by the people I care deeply about.

_____ 30. I am organized, plan my career carefully and set short-term and long-term goals.

_____ 31. I experience unpredictable mood swings from the highs of feeling elite and superior to the lows of depression and/or anger.

_____ 32. I am uncomfortable about sharing my feelings with other people. I would rather share my knowledge with other people.

—————— 33. I often doubt my own capabilities, even when I have performed well in the past and other people have praised me.

—————— 34. When I am bored or not doing something enjoyable, I immediately begin to plan for something enjoyable to do.

—————— 35. When someone does something unjust to me I get angry, and I want to "get even" by hurting them the way they hurt me.

—————— 36. I feel responsible for the welfare of other people, and I sacrifice myself to help people I care about live an effortless and comfortable life.

—————— 37. I am usually punctual and get irritated when other people are late.

—————— 38. I should come first in the lives of those close to me because I am so loving and helpful to them, even though I usually don't feel that I am first in their lives.

—————— 39. I work hard and play hard, and it's difficult for me to take a slow, relaxing vacation.

—————— 40. In my private thoughts I am often envious of other people.

—————— 41. I collect unusual items such as needles, confetti or barbed wire, and I have difficulty discarding anything.

—————— 42. In work situations and relationships I need to know exactly what others expect of me

_____ 43. I like to be active and around fun-loving people. As a result, some people mistakenly think that I am shallow.

_____ 44. I believe people cause their own problems by being weak and not standing up for themselves.

_____ 45. I just want to live a quiet, peaceful and worry-free life.

_____ 46. I often think about how to live the "right kind of life."

_____ 47. I am deeply hurt when someone I care about criticizes me. They should love me unconditionally.

_____ 48. I am adept in any social situation and can present a very admirable image.

_____ 49. The romances in my life have a tragic quality to them. I am often depressed about my previous romantic relationships.

_____ 50. I believe most people don't think as in depth or as carefully about important things as I do.

_____ 51. I am dutiful and reliable at work and in relationships.

_____ 52. I tend to be optimistic and see the good side of people.

_____ 53. I am direct with people, and I will confront people with whom I am upset. I don't like people who aren't direct with me.

_____ 54. I often have difficulty keeping my attention on what people are saying to me. My mind tends to wander.

_____ 55. I work hard because it is necessary to get things done right, not because it is fun.

_____ 56. I compliment people frequently, not so much to make them happy but to let them know that I care for them.

_____ 57. Lazy people really upset me.

_____ 58. People don't understand me, and so I need to express myself through art, acting, poetry, or some other form of creative outlet.

_____ 59. It is very difficult for people to win arguments with me because I am smart and only argue about things which I have studied thoroughly.

_____ 60. I am often cautious because I worry that other people will judge me unfairly.

_____ 61. I am optimistic about the future and always have plans for new and exciting things to do. And I always have backup plans.

_____ 62. I am aggressive and feel that the rules of society are for other people.

_____ 63. I try not to let other people or events in life upset or bother me.

TEST RESULTS

								Total	Type
1___	10___	19___	28___	37___	46___	55___	=	___	= **1**
2___	11___	20___	29___	38___	47___	56___	=	___	= **2**
3___	12___	21___	30___	39___	48___	57___	=	___	= **3**
4___	13___	22___	31___	40___	49___	58___	=	___	= **4**
5___	14___	23___	32___	41___	50___	59___	=	___	= **5**
6___	15___	24___	33___	42___	51___	60___	=	___	= **6**
7___	16___	25___	34___	43___	52___	61___	=	___	= **7**
8___	17___	26___	35___	44___	53___	62___	=	___	= **8**
9___	18___	27___	36___	45___	54___	63___	=	___	= **9**

Add the number of points horizontally. Match the *highest* total score on the right in the column labeled **Total**, to the number in the column to the far right marked **Type**. The corresponding number in the column marked **Type** is the most likely number of your Enneagram Type.

Even if several of your scores were close, use the highest score to determine your most likely type. Use this as a *beginning* for your self-discovery of your Enneagram type. The other high total scores can be used as secondary choices if you feel the highest score does not accurately identify your Enneagram type. Reading the brief descriptions of each type which follows and the next chapter, "Mistaken Identities," will help you either confirm your type or determine a more accurate one. If you need more information to determine your type, read the detailed descriptions of your most likely type in chapter six, seven and eight paying particular attention to how each type responds to stress and relaxation.

INTRODUCTION TO THE NINE ENNEAGRAM PERSONALITY TYPES

Now that you have completed the Enneagram Personality Test, you are ready to be introduced to the nine principal Enneagram Personality Types.

Before we explore the nine types, look at the Enneagram closely. Notice the arrangement of the types around the circle and the inner connecting lines. As you proceed in this book you will understand how the Enneagram helps you to know yourself, as well as provide you with precise knowledge about how the types relate to each other.

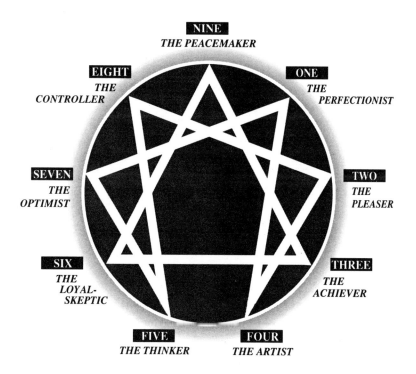

NINE
THE PEACEMAKER

EIGHT
THE CONTROLLER

ONE
THE PERFECTIONIST

SEVEN
THE OPTIMIST

TWO
THE PLEASER

SIX
THE LOYAL-SKEPTIC

THREE
THE ACHIEVER

FIVE
THE THINKER

FOUR
THE ARTIST

THE NINE PERSONALITY TYPES ON THE ENNEAGRAM

The descriptions which follow include the compelling desire (motivation), dominant avoidance (fear), persona (how we like to see ourselves and present ourselves to the world) and what special capacities we have to share with the world community for each personality type.

As we become more aware of ourselves, our enslavement to our avoidances and desires lessens, and we become more free, capable and content. Our persona softens, and our essence begins to emerge. We become more genuine, more fully human and begin to blossom.

Please realize that even though at different times in our lives we exhibit characteristics of all nine types, one type dominates our life, especially our close relationships. It is important to discover this primary personality type ("home base") because it has by far the greatest impact on our life. This primary personality type is where our unique gifts, defense mechanisms, perceptual distortions and desires are the strongest.

Type One: Perfectionists strive, by hard work, worry and preventive thinking, to avoid mistakes, to set high personal standards, and to "do the right thing." Their efforts to be flawless and to achieve personal ideals is an attempt to escape from their own inner-directed anger, self-criticism and guilt. This drive for perfection makes them feel resentful and angry. However, because they strive to be morally perfect, they generally don't display their anger to other people except as "helpful" criticism. They like to be seen as conscientious, disciplined, clear-thinking and efficient and, at a deep level, they are. Their special contributions to the world come from their exceptional self-discipline and high ideals.

Type Two: Pleasers take pride in being helpful, loving, and giving. They want to help other people feel "cared about" and thus to be seen as needed and indispensable. They seek to avoid feeling unloved, unneeded, separate and abandoned. They feel justified in using manipulation to get people to like and need them. They want others to see them as sweet, kind, and caring. And, at a deep level, they are. Their unique contributions to the world are their love and compassion.

Type Three: Achievers work hard to be successful or at least try to appear successful at whatever they do. When they appear productive and others see them as successful, they feel good and valued. Otherwise they tend to feel depressed and of little value. They want to avoid failure at all costs. They think about, talk about (often bragging), and spend most of their available time working to achieve success. They strive for others to see them as leaders, productive and successful. And, at a deep level, they have these capacities. Their unique gifts to the world are their determination and capacity to perform.

Type Four: Artists feel special and elite when they believe that they are unique, different, imaginative, and creative. If the elite or special feelings falter, artists tend to feel defective and rejected. Their mood swings from the high feelings associated with thinking that they are elite to the low depressive feelings of thinking that they are defective. Life to them is focused on creativity, nostalgia and the tragedy of the love that could have been or could be. They like to present an image of being creative, sensitive, emotionally deep and unique. And, at a deep level, they are. Their gifts to the world are creativity and aesthetics.

Type Five: Thinkers use their logic and objectivity to become expert in some specialized field of knowledge. They enjoy the process of learning and understanding things in great detail. They tend to avoid feelings, value privacy and are often withdrawn because they fear being overwhelmed by feelings. Thinkers like to be seen as experts, knowledgeable, methodical and socially aloof. Their special contribution to the world is their capacity for precise and detailed thinking.

Type Six: Loyal-Skeptics seek security by being careful, cautious and watchful. Predictability in jobs and relationships helps to make them feel secure. They don't like to deviate from set rules. They are loyal to people and organizations whom they can count on to have clear rules and philosophies. They procrastinate and become anxious or doubtful when faced with decisions or situations which are unclear. They tend to be suspicious of others and often develop a keen capacity to assess other people. They like to be seen as dutiful, loyal, dependable, and sometimes as brave and courageous. Their unique contributions to the world are their loyalty and capacity to be intuitive.

Type Seven: Optimists are curious, enthusiastic, fun-loving and feel things will always "work out for the best." They try to avoid boredom and pain. They are idealistic and have numerous plans for the future with optional back-up plans should the initial plan become too difficult or uninteresting. If their plans are interfered with they can become very angry and resentful. They project an image of being happy, flexible, adventurous and carefree. These attributes reflect their underlying capacities to uplift others and be joyous.

Type Eight: Controllers strive for power and control. They especially protect and want control over their life, emotions and personal "territory." They are arrogant, decisive, outspoken and feel justified in the excessive pursuit of what they want out of life. They want respect. If you cross them, they can be vengeful. They seek vengeance in the name of justice and as a way to avoid any feelings of weakness and vulnerability. They want people to see them as leaders: powerful, aggressive and determined. And they are. Their special contributions to the world are their power and courage.

Type Nine: Peacemakers try to go with the flow, often having to space out or deaden themselves in an effort to experience an untroubled life. They see all points of view, over-adjust to the desires of others and postpone decisions to avoid conflict and anger. They want to be viewed as humble, easygoing, nice, and accepting. And they usually are. Their unique contributions to the world are their capacities to be understanding and supportive.

WHAT DOES MY TYPE MEAN?

Now that you have a brief insight into the different personality types, you are ready to learn more about the meaning of personality and the Enneagram. The connection between your Enneagram Type and how you perceive the world will be introduced in this section.

Your personality is your tendency to think, feel and behave in a consistent manner over a long period of time and across a variety of situations. It is your identity, who you think you are. The Enneagram Personality Type, which you have or are beginning to identify after taking the self-test, explains your personality, its desires and fears, its strengths and weaknesses. Our personality determines how we view the world, and it satisfies our learned beliefs about how the world should be. The Enneagram not only describes how each personality type perceives the world, but also how each personality type acts in the world.

A word of Greek origin, Enneagram means "nine-pointed graph." The Enneagram groups people into nine interrelated categories or types according to their major *motivation* or *desire* and *perception.* Your motivation or desire determines where you place your energy for future achievement. Your perception – your awareness of your sensory environment as interpreted by your mind – determines your experience of the environment. So, what you do and what you see, hear, and even what you smell in your environment are all focused and shaped according to the way your personality type perceives. Therefore, even though our observable behavior many be very similar and we assume that we all see the world in the same way, we don't. Each of us lives in our own world with different motivations toward, and different perceptions of, the same environment.

There is an ancient Zen proverb which says that when pickpockets see someone, they only see the person's pockets. Like the pickpocket, we have limited perception, except instead of limiting our perception to only pockets, our perception is limited by our compelling desire. Depending upon our personality type, we see only those things which will help us succeed or make us feel secure or elite. And, like the pickpocket, we are unaware of the way we distort our life. It's as if we are each looking at the world through a unique stained-glass shell which surrounds us and blocks out or distorts our vision. Some of the glass is opaque and blocks our perception completely. Other parts of the glass are rose-colored and distort our perception in favor of optimism. And some of the glass is gray and makes the world look depressing.

Your compelling desire (pleasing, achieving, power or control) is the central driving force in your life. It represents your primary hope for love and happiness. Your compelling desire is fueled by what Freud called your unconscious and Jung called your shadow or "dark side". In this book the unconscious fear which specifically fuels your compelling desire is called your most dominant avoidance (fear). Your most dominant fear may be of abandonment, failure or rejection. The degree to which you are driven by your compelling desire reveals not only your desirable behavior but also how fearful you are of abandonment or failure or whatever your most dominant fear is.

Hard-working, successful business people are not very open to the idea that they are driven by fear in addition to their desire for excellence. Nor are you or I very open to the idea that fear is a major, unconscious, factor in what drives us to do what we do.

It requires courage to study the Enneagram because it exposes our total personality, including the dark side. On the other hand, it is *necessary* to face our dark side or most dominant avoidance (fear) if we are to understand the dynamics of our personality and free ourselves from its domination. It is *impossible* to achieve significant psychological growth without facing our unconscious fears.

As was mentioned in Chapter One, our Enneagram type is formed in our first few years of life and does not change over the course of our lifetime. The Enneagram allows us to discover our compelling desire which forms the foundation of our personality, our fixated way of living. It also provides a map for understanding how our personality responds while stressed or relaxed. And it offers specific guidelines for future personal growth. But remember - the map is not the territory - the Enneagram map does not exactly describe anyone's life in detail. Each of us is a unique individual. However, the Enneagram description and map do have enough detail and insight to last us through a lifetime of discovery and growth.

CHAPTER

3

MISTAKEN IDENTITIES

"We meet ourselves in a thousand disguises along the path."
- Plato

A t this point in the book, some readers aren't yet certain about which Enneagram type they are. Part of the problem is that some of us don't really want to know, and part of the problem is that the observable behavior for several types can look alike, even though their underlying motivations are different. For example, Type Eights, the Controllers, and Threes, the Achievers, look alike when they are both being efficient and working hard to succeed. The key to differentiating all Enneagram types lies in remembering that the types are based on what motivates a person, not on their observable behavior. Observable behavior can reflect many different underlying motivations.

The compelling desire for an Eight to be a leader is usually to obtain power and control, whereas the compelling drive for a Three is to feel successful and to gain the approval and admiration of other people. When striving to be leaders, both Eights and Threes may use or charm people. Eights use and charm people with the primary aim of feeling powerful. Threes use and charm people to be efficient and become successful leaders so they can feel looked up to, admired and valued by

27

other people.

Another reason some people are confused about their personality type is due to the characteristics inherent in their own personality type. Many times during workshops, Type Sixes, Loyal-Skeptics, will express uncertainty about their type. Part of being a Loyal-Skeptic is to be uncertain. Some Type Eights, Controllers, are resistant about being labeled because of their underlying fear that "if I can be typed, I can be controlled." Type Ones, Perfectionists, will often feel that they don't "perfectly" fit into any category. Nines, Peacemakers, because they can so readily understand other people better than themselves, often feel they fit in all categories equally and therefore not into just one category.

Some specific aspects of the confusion between several of the many possible personality type look-alikes are clarified in this chapter. They will help you examine and understand the similarities and differences between your Enneagram type and the other types which are most similar to your type.

TYPES TWO AND FOUR
THE PLEASER AND THE ARTIST

Both Type Two and Type Four personalities are very sensitive and can be very nurturing. Twos are generally nurturing and only get angry and demanding when they are stressed by the behavior of other people, which triggers within them feelings of rejection. In contrast, Fours, because of their mood swings, are sometimes nurturing and sometimes need to withdraw and be alone for no apparent reason. Fours are most nurturing when they are under stress.

TYPES ONE AND THREE
THE PERFECTIONIST AND THE ACHIEVER

Ones and Threes are both organized and efficient. However, the desire of Ones to be organized and efficient stems from their high ideals and fear of making mistakes. They feel that if they can avoid making mistakes, they can avoid being criticized or feeling guilty (criticized by the "inner critic") for wasting time and effort. They feel that it is "bad" to waste time. For Threes, it is a pragmatic need to be productive and to "get things done" that is the basis for their organized and efficient lives. They "love" to work, and they don't like to waste time and effort which could be better used to accomplish more.

Ones often procrastinate because of their need to make the one and only one "right" decision. Threes rush decision making to "get things done." Ones continuously strive to improve and be perfect and rarely feel like they have achieved perfection. Threes need to feel like a success even while they are striving for success and even if they aren't actually successful. This is one of the reasons why Threes call work fun. As long as they are being productive and feel like work is fun, they feel at least somewhat successful.

TYPES TWO AND SIX
THE PLEASER AND THE LOYAL-SKEPTIC

Twos and many Sixes can be confused with each other because they are both very personable and charming. However, the charm of the Twos is driven by their compelling desire to please because they want to feel needed. Sixes please to gain approval, validation, support and protection.

TYPES THREE AND EIGHT
THE ACHIEVER AND THE CONTROLLER

These two types were discussed briefly in the introduction to this chapter. Some additional differences between Types Three and Eight are: Threes like and tolerate tight schedules more than Eights do, and Threes work hard and "like" to work hard, whereas Eights will work hard only if it is necessary to achieve power or control over their environment.

TYPES FOUR AND THREE
THE ARTIST AND THE ACHIEVER

Fours seek to be elite and Threes seek to feel successful, seemingly very similar goals. However, the eliteness of the Fours set them apart from other people and is usually experienced privately in their own mind. They don't need the approval of others to feel elite. In fact, being approved of by others may undermine their feelings of eliteness unless they view the people who are approving them as also elite. In contrast, to feel successful Threes usually want public visibility, admiration and recognition.

TYPES FIVE AND NINE
THE THINKER AND THE PEACEMAKER

Nines easily identify with all types, and frequently mis-identify themselves as a Type Five. Nines also like to think; however, the style of their thinking is different. Nines think in generalities, frequently daydream and are less likely to pursue their lines of thought to completion. Fives, on the other hand, think in detail and like to pursue their line of thought to the most advanced point.

Both Nines and Fives like to spend time by themselves to

think. However, Fives have a greater need for privacy and seek it more aggressively.

TYPES SIX AND ONE
THE LOYAL-SKEPTIC AND
THE PERFECTIONIST

Sixes and Ones are both very submissive to authority and yet they are paradoxically often very bossy. Sixes tell others what to do to get them to comply to legal or organizational rules. Ones lecture others on what to do to get them to comply with what they perceive as the way everyone with high standards "should" be, or to make them perfect in the image of the Type One.

Both Sixes and Ones worry about the future. Sixes worry about the future in an attempt to reduce uncertainty in their lives. Ones worry about the future in an attempt to avoid mistakes which could lead to criticism and guilt from their inner critic. Both Ones and Sixes often wake up with a "thinking hangover." They stay awake too late, thinking and worrying and then aren't alert and able to function to their full capacity the following morning.

TYPES SEVEN AND ONE
THE OPTIMIST AND THE PERFECTIONIST

Both Sevens and Ones plan for the future. Sevens plan fun activities which they can easily abandon if the activity doesn't turn out to be fun, and they always have at least one backup plan. Ones take their plans much more seriously and feel compelled to properly complete exactly what they originally planned to do. They postpone their fun until after their "serious" plans have been completed. Many Type Ones never finish their "serious" pursuits and don't ever find time to have fun during their lifetime!

CHAPTER

4

THE "BEST" PERSONALITY TYPES

A seeker entered a forest which was full of sickly, drooping and unstable trees. He asked a drooping pine tree why it was so droopy. The pine tree responded, "I am sad and depressed because I always wanted to be a birch tree. It is so graceful and powerful looking." Next he came upon a birch tree which was shaking, standing rigid and looking quite menacing. He asked the birch tree why it was so angry. The birch tree responded, "I am so angry because I have never liked being a birch tree. I would not be so angry if I were a liquid amber tree; the colors of its leaves in the fall are magnificent."

Most of the trees in the forest were sickly to the trained eye of the seeker. He was surprised when he came upon a weeping willow tree which was healthy and radiant. When asked why she was so radiant, the weeping willow said, "After struggling for a long time to be something which I am not and draining myself of energy, I gave up and decided that I could be nothing more than what I am. Since that time I have tried to be the best weeping willow that I can. Now, my heart is at ease, my being is radiant, and I am at peace."

If we are to grow and flourish, we need to acknowledge and accept who we are. As we do, we will also grow in knowledge and acceptance of others for who they are. We won't expect them to be something different than what they are. We will stop expecting to get apples from an orange tree. We will discover there *is* no best personality type!

Through discovering and accepting your own unique personality, you can begin to become all that you are capable of becoming. Don't focus your energy on determining which is the right personality type for you or someone else. Realize and accept that *everyone* is fixated in different personality types and each personality type contributes to the world in its own unique way. Acceptance and understanding of yourself and others leads to a more peaceful and loving life. When you reduce unreasonable expectations of yourself and others, your relationship with yourself and others becomes clearer and more enjoyable.

As you become more self-aware, you may begin to realize that you are the world, even though you function from day to day with your own unique personality type. At some level and to some degree, we all have characteristics of Hitler and Mother Theresa within us. This realization can be upsetting, or it can open you to deeper self-understanding and self-acceptance, and greater acceptance and compassion for others.

Your personality includes all of the personality types on the Enneagram. What makes you unique and different is how much of each personality type you have within you and which type is your "home base." Depending upon your mood and the particular situation in which you find yourself, you temporarily behave like other personality types. For example, if you are a Type Five, Thinker, and are around a helpless young child, the pleasing, helpful nature of a Type Two, Pleaser, may emerge temporarily within you. So, in effect, you are comprised of the characteristics of many personalities.

Understanding and accepting your personality type leads to a reduction in unreasonable expectations of yourself and others. It frees a lot of the energy we tie up in guilt, anger and depression, which leads to better relationships and a more enjoyable life.

Knowing and accepting your personality type helps you

understand your strengths and weaknesses. Everyone has them, and everyone has what society calls assets and liabilities. It is as important to know your weaknesses and liabilities as it is to know your strengths and assets. If you repress or ignore your weaknesses and liabilities, they won't go away. They will likely undermine your efforts to utilize your strengths and assets. Acknowledging your weaknesses and liabilities and accepting them allows you to see them more clearly, work around them and more readily achieve your personal potential.

PART 2

DEEPENING, INTEGRATING, AND LOVING

PART TWO
DEEPENING, INTEGRATING AND LOVE

"The unexamined life is not worth living."
- Socrates

In the last chapter I posed the question about which Enneagram type is best or contributes the most to the world. The answer was that they are all equal and all have a special contribution to make to the world. If the question is who is most healthy, happy, fulfilled or has the most loving relationships, the answer is still the same. No particular type is any healthier than any other. No matter what your Enneagram type is, the only way you can become more healthy is by becoming more awake and free. The frog and scorpion mentioned in Chapter One are both stuck and they can't change. You and I aren't stuck - we can grow and expand. To the extent we grow and expand, we become more healthy, our sense of well-being improves, our relationships are enhanced and we contribute more to the world.

Love is knowing yourself intimately. So, the better you know yourself, the better you will love yourself and others. You will grow and deepen self-understanding. Discovering your Enneagram type as you did in Part One is rewarding and exciting. Part Two is designed to help you use this excitement to move into a deeper, clearer understanding of yourself, your childhood and your relationships. It will help you: (1) gain a deeper, more detailed understanding of your specific personality type; (2) understand why people are attracted to each other; (3) determine what Enneagram types they are most attracted to; (4) know how to relate well with other personality types; (5) learn how your personality type was developed; and (6) become aware of specific recommendations for the personal growth of your own personality type.

Chapter Six presents details on Enneagram Types Two, Three,

and Four. Chapter Seven presents details on Types Five, Six, and Seven. Chapter Eight presents details on types Eight, Nine and One. If you are still unsure about your type, read the details about the most likely other types, remembering that the underlying compelling desire is the deciding factor in the differences between types.

But remember that words and concepts, no matter how clear or accurate, can only take you so far in understanding Enneagram personality types. While this book and the books in the bibliography are extremely valuable introductions to the Enneagram, to fully appreciate and understand the Enneagram it is *necessary* to experience each type as they present themselves in a group situation.

When you meet people who have the same personality type in a group situation, you will first be blinded by the differences in their age, sex, cultural background and lifestyle. However, in a very brief period of time you will be amazed at the underlying similarities in thinking and emotional expression which are characteristic of their same Enneagram personality type.

For more depth of understanding and greater clarity of your own personality type, take a workshop on the Enneagram. If this isn't possible, find two or three people with your same personality type and share with each other your reactions to the detailed information about your type as outlined in Part Two of this book. It will be an enjoyable and informative experience. A workshop or sharing with your same personality type will be a giant step in your belief and understanding of the power and accuracy of the Enneagram.

CHAPTER
5

DESIRE AND MORE

"When you are no longer compelled by desire or fear ... when you follow your bliss ... doors will open where you would not have thought there were doors ... and the world will step in and help."
- Joseph Campbell

B efore we focus on the personality types individually, terms which are used throughout the descriptions of Enneagram types need to be reviewed. These terms include "compelling desire," "associated desires," "wings," "stress response," "relaxation response," "sub-types," and "recognition."

COMPELLING DESIRE

Various authors and teachers have labeled this component of the Enneagram personality type description as the character fixation, passion, programming, compulsion, addiction, preoccupation, or idealization. I decided to use the term compelling desire because for me the word compel perfectly expresses the forcefulness and irresistibility of this drive.

The word desire refers to something which promises

enjoyment or satisfaction in its attainment. The compelling desire is what motivates people to "do" what they "do" in life. As Aristotle said, the nature of desire is that it cannot be satisfied even though you may live your life for its gratification. The compelling desire is the *central driving force* in your life, and it represents your primary hope for enjoyment and satisfaction.

This desire is based upon the avoidance of a deep fear (lack of basic trust) which developed in childhood. Chapter Nine will provide greater depth of understanding about your compelling desire and how it relates to your personality development. What's important to remember here is that, because the compelling desire is an avoidance of fear, the intensity of your compelling desire reflects the intensity of your avoidance of fear, which in turn reflects how trustworthy and nurturing your environment was in childhood. For example: a Type Two who wants to please very much had a less nurturing childhood environment, is driven by a greater fear of abandonment, and experiences a greater blocking of their strength and loving nature than a Type Two whose desire to please is less intense.

I chose the word desire because it also ties into the process of transformation. Although it may not make sense to you now, after you finish Part Two of this book you will be aware of how lessening fixated desires of any kind results in less fear. Or, it could be said that when you are less fearful, you have fewer and less intense fixated desires. When your fears and desires lessen, you will be less constricted. You will have a greater amount of free energy to live life in a full and rewarding manner and you will have greater access to your essence. You will become even less fearful. And, as Joseph Campbell wrote, "...you will follow your bliss."

In many strategies of transformation, *any* desire is considered to ultimately interfere with the highest levels of growth and transformation. All desires are considered to fixate your attention on the future and limit your field of perception. But what about the desire for love and truth? Certainly these desires are essential!

At the stage of development that most of us are currently at in our lives, it is certainly reasonable and helpful to desire love and truth. And these desires will enhance the growth process. Ultimately, however, at very advanced stages of transformation, even desiring love and truth will cease because love and truth will emerge from your essence not from your fixated desires. Love and truth will permeate your personality, your relationships and your entire life.

ASSOCIATED DESIRES

For each compelling desire, several associated desires are described. Each of these associated desires are spinoffs or subsets of the compelling desire. The compelling desire puts into motion a pattern of related psychodynamics in each particular personality type. For example, the compelling desire for a Type Nine, the Peacemaker, is to have a peaceful life. Associated with this compelling desire for peace are desires to avoid anger, avoid conflict, maintain the status quo, change slowly and merge with others.

WINGS

Your Wings are the personality types on either side of your Enneagram type. The Wings for Type Two are Type One and Type Three. The Wings for a Nine are One and Eight. Using the Type Two as an example, some Twos lean toward or are more influenced by the One Wing and thus are more perfectionistic than other Twos. But some Twos lean toward the Three Wing and are thus more achievement oriented. The important thing to remember is that the similarity between all Twos is far greater than their differences. However, the differences based on their Wings is very significant.

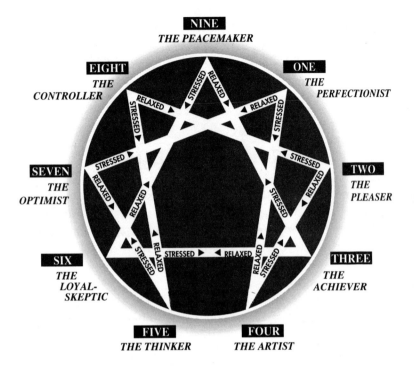

STRESS AND RELAXATION RESPONSES

The connecting lines on the Enneagram represent relationships between personality types. Although, movement to different points (types) on the Enneagram occurs when you become stressed or relaxed, **you don't change your personality type and your compelling desire remains the same**. However, your strategy for achieving your compelling desire changes. Stress moves you along the connecting line with the arrow labeled **(STRESSED)**. Relaxation, which in Enneagram theory is the awareness of being loved, moves you along the connecting line labeled **(RELAXED)**. For example, Twos, Pleasers, behave like an Eight, Controller, under stress. They become angry and remind you of all the things that they have done for you and how you have done so little for them in return. But, when relaxed, Twos act like Fours, Artists. They become extra-sensitive to rejection and expect tragedy in their romantic life.

SUB-TYPES

Each personality type can be subdivided into three sub-types. These sub-types focus on issues of self-preservation, social relationships or intimate relationships. Each particular personality type will exhibit the characteristics of all three sub-types but will tend to be dominated by one of the three sub-types more than the others. So, when each personality type is subdivided into its three sub-types, the Enneagram identifies nine times three or twenty-seven personality types. However, the differences in the personalities of sub-types is much less than the differences in the personalities of the nine primary personality types, since each sub-type maintains the same compelling desire as the primary type. The sub-type descriptions in this book are more tentative than that of the primary types and are being researched and explored more in my ongoing work with the Enneagram.

RECOGNIZING TYPES

Everyone in a particular personality type does not dress or behave the same, even though their underlying desires are very similar. For example, all Fours dislike being ordinary. So when you see someone who dresses in unusual and different clothes, they are more likely to be a Type Four than any other personality type. However, some Type Fours feel elite by dressing very, very ordinary (extra ordinary). In general though, there are similarities in the dress, eyes and verbal expressions of each type. The recognition profile that is presented for each type is *representative* of the type and does not fit every individual in the type.

PEOPLE OF THE HEART

THE HEART CENTER
TYPES TWO, THREE AND FOUR

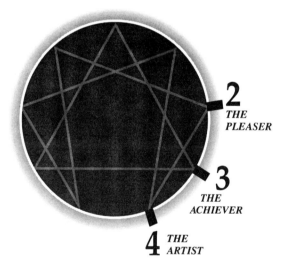

2
THE
PLEASER

3
THE
ACHIEVER

4 *THE*
ARTIST

Twos, Threes, and Fours are clustered in what is called the
heart center. The heart center includes those personality
types which are primarily motivated by heartfelt
emotions such as love, and by the avoidance of injuries to the
heart. Injuries to the heart center are usually felt emotionally as

47

depression. Paradoxically, the Type Three personalities are at the center of the heart center and are only moderately in contact with their heartfelt emotions. However, like the other heart center types, Threes experience depression when the image they hope will be admired (loved) isn't acknowledged.

Projecting a lovable image is important to the heart center people because, at an unconscious level, they believe they are not loveable for who they really are. However, at a still deeper level, their loving nature is attempting to reveal itself. Twos seek love by being helpful and pleasing. Threes seek love by gaining respect and admiration for their achievements and successes. The Fours try to be lovable by being unique and original.

These three types, the heart center, focus their concerns on what other people think of them and feel about them. They want other people to need them, admire their work, or see their uniqueness. Because they focus so much attention on image, they tend to be very concerned about their outer appearance.

This group also seeks love and acceptance by being with the "right" person. For example, a success-oriented Three will often seek partners who provide them with the best image for success, rather than an intimate relationship. Fours seek to be with other "elite" people.

Threes exhibit much less emotion than the other types in this group, and they are somewhat detached from their bodies. In fact, Threes frequently over-stress their bodies because they view them as vehicles to be used for success rather than as something to be nurtured.

At first glance, it's difficult to understand how Threes could be motivated by the heart center when actually their heartfelt feelings are more repressed than Types Two and Four. Threes are attached to the heart center because their underlying loving nature is trying to emerge and paradoxically their compelling desire to achieve causes them to *avoid* the heart by not being very concerned about the need for love. Heartfelt feelings interfere with achievement. Twos and Fours "go along" with their heartfelt emotions, whereas the Threes avoid and repress their heartfelt emotions. Whether you avoid or go along with something, you are controlled by it. Teenagers who "go along" with their parents' wishes and teenagers who rebel and do the opposite of what their parents wish are both controlled by their parents.

THE PLEASER TYPE TWO

"I'll do it for you...It's no problem...Wait, let me do it...Your life would be better if you would...I got this for you...I did this for you...I made this for you." These phrases are repeated over and over again by Twos. Behind these pleasing phrases are cries for love, acceptance and a fervent desire to be needed. Twos are the over-working and self-sacrificing mothers, assistants, secretaries, husbands and wives.

The **compelling desire** for a Two is to please everyone around them and thus to feel important, needed, and loved. Giving is their primary form of pleasing. To express their love and to gain acceptance, praise and approval, they give advice, gifts, and compliments. They feel good and lovable when they please and make others feel cared for.

To the outside observer they appear happy and content. They are loved and appreciated for their self-sacrificing ways. However, this love is dependent on their capacity to please and on having someone to please. Inside, they remain anxious that they aren't doing enough and that the people they serve will abandon them. The people Twos serve can rarely and only momentarily reassure Twos that they are loved and valued.

As with compelling desires for all personality types, a never-ending circle of hope which will never produce the desired results is lived out. In the case of Twos, they repress and reject their own need for love and give the love that they desire to others. When they don't get the love they hoped for in return, they feel an even greater need for love. So, they repress their love need even more and hope to get it from others who will love them because they give so much love. And so the never-ending, only momentarily fulfilling, circle continues.

In fact, Twos who devote the most energy to pleasing repress their own need for love the most and are the least healthy. Because their pleasing is driven by the greatest desire to be loved and needed, they expend more effort and energy than others in order to please which leads to less energy and awareness available to fulfill their own real needs and an even greater fear of abandonment.

Don't judge the Twos!!! We are all on a similar merry-go-round which will never get us where we want to go! In Chapter Eleven and Part Three of this book, some of the things you can do to get off the merry-go-round are explored.

ASSOCIATED DESIRES

Connected with the compelling desire of the Type Two are a host of associated desires. We'll examine five of the most important associated desires: the desire for a life based on love, the desire to feel needed, the desire to avoid criticism, the desire to nurture, and the desire to feel proud.

A LIFE BASED ON LOVE

Love is everything to a Two. They want to feel loved and to help others feel loved and cared about. "When I love someone I tell them and show them over and over again. In return, I need my boyfriend to think the world of me."

Twos don't want to experience or give superficial love. They want unconditional heartfelt love. They crave an intimacy based on sharing their deepest feelings with other people. In fact, people are often surprised at the amount of information they reveal about their personal life to a Two during a brief, first-time meeting. "Love symbolizes togetherness and caring. Communication is security and honesty. When receiving love, security and honesty, I feel safe and warm; giving these, I feel whole and happy."

Twos tend to think with their heart instead of their head. When they say or do something with a loving intention, regardless of its logic, they expect people to be accepting and appreciative. For example, a Two may give gifts or make recommendations, based on their loving feelings, to people who may not want or feel comfortable in receiving them, and then be surprised when they are rejected or criticized for what they did.

Their often desperate need for love can cause them to be manipulative and possessive in order to get their way. "I get manipulative when I'm trying to win the affection of another person. Possessiveness is also a quality I am not proud of. Sometimes I can't seem to let go of a person; I hang on until there is nothing to hang on to." It is difficult for many Twos to recognize their own manipulative behavior because of their pride and the feeling that anything done in the name of love is right.

Twos tend to have an all-or-nothing attitude toward relationships. "I will love you totally and wait on you hand and foot. I can make any relationship work. However, if you don't love me or appreciate me, then I don't want to have anything to do with you."

FEELING NEEDED

Twos desire to feel needed is based on a deep fear of abandonment. "If I don't feel needed, I feel inadequate." Their desire to be needed causes them to deny and, in fact, be unaware of, their own personal needs. Consequently, Twos are very dependent on other people for their own sense of well-being.

Twos are also dependent on others for help in making decisions and setting limits on their personal behavior, for example how much they should get involved in a relationship, how much money they should spend, how much time to allot and many other aspects of their life. It is ironic that on the one hand, when others set limits for them it makes them feel "cared" for and protected. On the other hand, they resent others setting limits for them.

Even though they find it difficult to take care of their own emotional needs, Twos are often hedonistic and can be ardent shoppers. Many feel entitled to hedonistic behavior because they feel that they sacrifice so much for others. However, because they feel they might be abandoned if they have personal needs, they justify or rationalize that their purchases are actually for someone else or due to the needs of someone else.

Because of their strong need to be needed, Twos need to be viewed and to see themselves as giving and pleasing. They believe that they aren't supposed to have needs of their own. Therefore, it is hard for them to admit that they are capable of having selfish or self-centered desires. They often use subtle manipulations to keep other people from abandoning them. They take pride in the belief that they can make any relationship work, and will often do almost anything to sustain it.

Twos are sweet, give compliments and gifts, and are seductive, all to be helpful and to feel needed. Paradoxically, because they don't take care of their own needs and completely adapt themselves to the needs of others, they themselves are actually the needy ones. It is extremely difficult to reassure Twos except by constantly letting them know they are needed, valued and desired.

For example, if you tell a Two "I love you," they love it. However, because it's from an outside source which can't make up for their own lack of essential love, they need to be told over and over again that they are loved. Other people often feel drained by this need/demand for constant reassurance, and begin to feel burdened or withdraw.

Twos not only notice others' needs, they anticipate their needs. They will often offer help or advice before the other person even realizes that they need or want it. Believing that everyone else has the same capabilities, they expect other people to "see into" their heart and to know their needs. As a result, Twos are often disappointed at what they interpret as a lack of caring and compassion in the world by others, particularly when they feel it is directed toward themselves.

AVOID CRITICISM

When Twos don't feel needed, they feel very anxious, insecure and depressed. And the smallest rejection can trigger the fear of abandonment. Twos don't just feel bad, they "bleed" emotionally and become extremely anxious. "All my husband has to do is say the coffee is not hot enough and I start thinking he doesn't like my coffee so he must not like me. Obviously he probably never liked me. He's going to leave me."

The slightest criticism or lack of attention can cause a Two to feel hurt, so they tend to avoid confrontation. It's impossible to understate the hurt that Twos feel when they feel rejected or sense even the most innocent criticism. "I feel hurt if my parents say that they love me and then say, 'but of course you should know that!'."

Even though Twos are sensitive to criticism, they will risk criticism of themselves and confront other people if they feel that the confrontation is for protection of someone they care about. For example, many sweet, Type Two mothers will risk criticism and fiercely confront their child's school principal if they feel that their child is being treated unfairly.

NURTURING

Twos don't know their own needs very well. However, they are extremely capable at recognizing both the deep emotional needs and the more superficial daily needs of other people. They move toward other people and give nurturance in the form of helpful advice, gifts, compliments and flattery. The extent that nurturing and giving influences their life is apparent in this Type Two's statement: " I adjust my personality to please everyone. But, more important, I adjust much more than my personality - I adjust my life, my mood, my styles, my dress, my attitude, my beliefs, my morals, my voice, my goals, my likes (and dislikes). In other words, every part of me that you see is quite possibly temporary. And everything I give to you, including my attitude, is only what I believe I think you want from me." The effect of Two's desire to please and nurture important people in their life is evident in this effort to change not only more superficial components as mood or style of dress, but even more significant characteristics as attitude, morals, and goals. This Two's primary desire permeates its entire life.

Some well-known examples of Type Two personalities are Mr. Rogers, the television personality, and Elvis Presley, who revealed his Type Two tendencies by giving expensive and frequent gifts to fans and friends.

On the negative side, this constant giving is often egocentric. It is for personal pride, recognition and most importantly to feel needed and to get love in return. But Twos often feel angry and depressed because they believe that no one does or can ever return the amount of love and nurturing which Twos give. One Type Two said, "I sometimes feel that I get back only a minute part of the love I give." This experience can lead to feelings of being a victim and being used by other people.

Their nurturing also usually involves placing other people before themselves. "If someone else is feeling low, I will forget my problems and concentrate on theirs." And they don't just put one person first. If they are in a family or in some larger group such as a church, they will try to make the whole church or family feel nurtured. This over-nurturing "drains the life out of me," as one Two said, "...and causes me physical exhaustion and physical illness."

Twos have the strongest sense of empathy of all the personality types. They are attracted to people who are in need: children, old people, and people who need someone to support them emotionally. "I am drawn to people who need me and I would do anything for the people I love," wrote one Type Two. People in need are unlikely to reject Twos. When they enter a group situation, Twos almost always do a quick scan of the group to see which person looks like they may need nurturing.

Twos are enjoyable to be around. As a Type Two reported, "Most people I meet seem comfortable about talking to me and I enjoy being a listener and shoulder to lean on. At times I feel I have a sixth sense about when to listen and when to make suggestions. I think this is because it makes me feel needed."

PRIDE

Twos are proud of their loving nature, their giving and pleasing ways and usually take pride in their personal appearance. Their pride extends to the people whom they relate to. They like to associate with attractive and successful people.

Unfortunately, this pride leads them to feel privileged and deserving. Feeling that they are special and not wanting to openly appear to be needy of love leads Twos to manipulate others as a way to get what they really want - love.

Pride can make Twos try harder at all their efforts to please and feel wanted. Pride also keeps Twos from getting their own needs met. "I am embarrassed to have needs," wrote one Two. Another reports that she "never asks for anything." Twos have difficulty in asking for help, admitting that they can't handle a situation or recognizing that they have needs of any kind except the need to be loved. This can also be seen as a difficulty in admitting they have needs just like "ordinary people" have.

WINGS OF A TWO

(Wings are the Enneagram types on both sides of your number on the Enneagram)

REMEMBER, OUR PRIMARY DESIRE DOES NOT CHANGE WHEN WE LEAN TOWARD EITHER WING. HOWEVER, THE LEANING DOES INFLUENCE HOW WE SEEK TO ACHIEVE OUR COMPELLING DESIRE.

A Two who leans toward their Type One Wing is overly judgmental and perfectionistic. Their giving includes a lot of recommendations for reform and improvement. Their prideful needs are exacerbated by the perfectionist's need to be perfect, and their need to be loveable is exacerbated by needing to be perfect to be loveable.

Twos are often the personality types that assist and support successful people. They are excellent assistants for strong leaders. However, Twos leaning toward their Three Wing exhibit some achievement needs of their own and are often more motivated to achieve than other Twos.

When a Two doesn't lean toward either wing and is influenced equally by the One Wing and Three Wing concurrently, conflict arises between achieving by just getting things done, as Threes often do without too much consideration for quality, and wanting to work on things until they are perfected, like Ones.

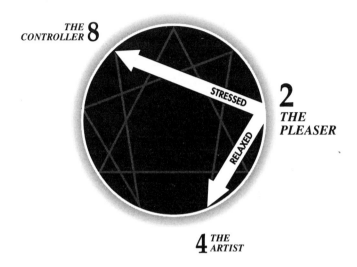

THE CONTROLLER **8**

STRESSED

RELAXED

2
THE PLEASER

4 *THE ARTIST*

STRESS AND RELAXATION

When Type Two personalities get **STRESSED** they move to a type Eight on the Enneagram. One Type Two said that her grandmother, who knew her very well, described her using an old nursery rhyme: "There was a little girl who had a little curl right in the middle of her forehead. And when she was good, she was very, very good, but when she was bad she was horrid." When Twos get upset, usually due to something that seems like it could lead to abandonment, they either become overwhelmed with sadness or anxiety, or their disowned anger breaks through, and as in this rhyme they move to the Eight position on the Enneagram and become angry, demanding, and self-righteous.

When Twos move to the Eight Point, they are "fragmented" and become so identified with their self-righteous anger that they can't be reasoned with. They feel that they deserve to be treated better because of how "good" they have been to others. One Type Two reported, "When I become stressed or angry, I definitely become an Eight, a Controller. I become very demanding and stubborn and will not cooperate with anyone until they see things my way." After the outburst, they usually apologize and immediately intensify their efforts to be loved by pleasing and giving even more than they did before.

When Type Two personalities are **RELAXED** they move to a Type Four on the Enneagram. Twos are not generally as artistic as Fours. However, when they feel relaxed and good, their energy is often channeled into the creative outlets of the Four.

Also, when Twos are feeling especially relaxed and good, it is usually because they are feeling extra needed and loved. But now, they may experience increased fears of abandonment because now they have "even more love to risk losing." So, when they feel too good, they tend to be more sensitive than normal and expect something to go wrong. "Our love is too good to be true." They are paradoxically more difficult to get close to during this time of ultra-sensitivity. Sometimes this makes it impossible for their partner to give them what they crave - love. And, like a Four, they experience tragic, depressing feelings for the love that could have been or might never be in the future.

Recognizing a Representative Type Two Personality

Twos are seen as the ultimate kind, caring and giving person. They are soft-spoken and charming. They are "soft" looking and exhibit little muscular "holding" in their bodies. They speak somewhat like an elementary school teacher might speak to their students: helpful, reassuring and gentle. They easily and quickly establish rapport with people. They are very friendly and approachable and subtly pull people to them. They tend to take pride in their physical appearance.

SUB-TYPES OF TYPE TWO

Type Twos can be subdivided into three sub-types, allowing a more specific understanding of Type Twos. In the life of some Type Twos, intimate relationships are dominant. In others, social relationships are most important. Yet for other Twos, self-preservation issues are dominant.

INTIMATE RELATIONSHIPS: AGGRESSIVE SEDUCTION

These Twos are some of the most seductive people on the Enneagram. They love to flirt, especially with people whom they perceive as powerful. They enter a room, sense where the power is, and move to seduce it. The seduction tends to be a combination of charm and sexuality. The object is not necessarily sexual contact per se, but to know that they are wanted, approved of and will be taken care of. As a result, they are often accused of being teasers. Seductive Twos like to make physical contact, even if it's just a gentle touch or pat on the shoulder.

SOCIAL RELATIONSHIPS: AMBITION

Social Relationship sub-types focus on becoming close to or associating with powerful or high-status people. One Type Two said, "I am socially ambitious. I can walk into a crowded room, identify the people with the most power, approach them, say just the right things to impress them and get them to believe in me. An example is when I went to work at a major corporation. I learned immediately how to get close to key players within the company. These people were my stability; in essence, my backbone. It is scary to think of how much power I actually possessed by being nice."

SELF-PRESERVATION: PRIVILEGE

Twos give excessively and often sacrifice their own needs. They work hard to make other people feel loved and cared for.

As a result of their self-sacrifice, Self-Preservation Twos expect to be treated as privileged. They feel justified and entitled to receive special treatment such as extra service in a restaurant, having people they are meeting wait for them, spending extra money on themselves or cutting in front of others in a line.

THE ACHIEVER
TYPE THREE

"It's how much money you have that really counts...It's not what you do, but who you know that counts...I've got two jobs, and I am going to night school and I love it...Go for it...Don't call me a workaholic – I love to work hard...I did it on my own... Feelings get in the way of success..." Three is the personality type which our culture holds up as the ideal. Threes, along with Type Eight and Type One personalities, are the salespeople, leaders and producers in our society. They are competitive, work hard, look appropriate and strive to feel successful.

Threes are at the core or central point on the Enneagram for the heart center. Twos and Fours on either side are easily recognized as emotional and sensitive. But Threes are not very emotionally sensitive. Their emotions tend to be superficial, in contrast to the deeply felt emotions of the Twos and Fours. Their goal in life is to be efficient and to achieve, and to do that they must avoid heartfelt emotions. Emotions get in the way of the need to produce and become successful. One Type Three reported, "I am emotionally sensitive, but I stuff my feelings deep down inside to avoid hurt, then I move down the road to new projects and prospects."

However, like the Twos and the Fours, Threes experience depression when their compelling desire is not fulfilled. Donald Trump is a famous Type Three personality.

The **compelling desire** of Threes is to be recognized as successful at whatever they do. They are preoccupied with marketing themselves, appearing successful and often bragging about their success. "Achievement gives me an 'adrenaline rush,'" explained one Type Three. Their hard work is aimed at avoiding their dark side, which is the fear of failure and blocked inner sense of value. If they're not productive and successful, they feel worthless and depressed.

Even acknowledging fear of failure feels "unsuccessful" to a Type Three. So, as one Type Three put it, "I am not afraid of failure. I don't fail. I have 'setbacks' which I learn from and they help me to become more successful."

Threes can never produce enough, achieve enough or get enough admiration. They're constantly running toward another goal or achievement – the reward behind the reward is adulation, admiration, and being valued by *others*. This is a substitute for self-worth and love.

ASSOCIATED DESIRES

The four associated desires for the Type Three personality are the desire to feel successful, to be a hard worker, to be efficient and to be socially admired.

TO FEEL SUCCESSFUL

Threes are so identified with their achievement that only if things are going successfully at work do they feel good. If things aren't going well at work, they feel bad. A majority of the stockbrokers who jumped out of windows when the stock market crashed in the Thirties were Threes. The market failed. They failed.

To help themselves feel like winners and become winners, Threes like to associate with, admire and copy other Achievers. They enjoy vicariously experiencing and identifying with the successes of successful people. For example, business leaders are often Type Threes and generally identify more with the success and failure of sports teams than other personality types.

In their quest to feel successful, emotions – whether their own emotions and fear or other people's emotions – are viewed as obstacles to be avoided or overcome. As a result, Threes can be ruthless, manipulative and insensitive. "I am getting married because the company I work for views a good wife as an asset for its managers. I am willing to put a lot of time into the relationship now because it is necessary. The time requirement for my relationship after I am married should diminish, and I can return my focus to my work." When this Type Three was asked what he would do if his wife demanded too much of his time after they were married, he replied matter-of-factly that he would "terminate" the relationship. The Type Twos in the workshop gasped when they heard this response.

Failure is to be avoided. If it occurs, it is ignored or rationalized so that the feeling of success can be maintained at all cost. It is almost as if their brain has a malfunction in the part that records and recalls failure. In fact, research on memory indicates that we store and recall information in our memory according to what fits our self-concept.

To Be A Hard Worker

Their bodies are vehicles for success. When Threes take time out from work to exercise, it is to become stronger and to increase productivity. Work is what they like most in life. Vacations are taken at "in" locations for their image and/or to help their body recover and become more productive – not for fun or relaxation. One Type Three called vacations a "waste of time." Another Three remarked, "When I am not working, I don't know what to do." Their sense of worth is based on being productive and doing things. When they relax, they feel worthless. In addition, a nonproductive vacation creates "space" in their life where emotions might enter. Emotions are "uncomfortable" and could interfere with future productivity.

As a result of working hard, Threes often burn out psychologically or wear out their bodies. As one remarked, "I have to really feel sick to stop working. By that time I usually end up in the hospital." A trip to the hospital usually only slows down a Three temporarily, even when they have suffered a heart attack which is clearly related to their compulsion of working too hard. As soon as they are out of the hospital or even while still in the hospital, they are driven to resume their demanding work schedule.

Because their sense of self-worth is so tied to accomplishing tasks successfully, they are often viewed as workaholics. One Three reported, "I often find myself at work after everyone else has left, trying to finish 'just one last thing.' People have called me a 'workaholic.' I just want to know that I'm appreciated for the work I do. Even though I know how hard I work, I'm always trying to do more. So, in other words, I may be obsessed with the feeling of complete failure if I'm not performing at my absolute best."

A Three related, "I worked hard seven days a week before I got married. I loved my wife and felt it was important that I spend more time with her. However, every time I did, I got severe headaches. The solution we found in order to have time together was for her to work with me. I couldn't stop working!" Hard work to a Three is like a drug to a drug addict. "I get a great deal of stimulation from being successful and productive; the more I accomplish the higher I get."

I remember one new client of mine who was a Type Three. She was proud that she could work six days a week for twelve hours a day. Her concern was that on the seventh day she was exhausted, severely depressed and anxious. She told me on the first visit that she wanted to feel better on the seventh day but continue to work the same intense, long hours for the other six days. I told her we would need to examine her entire week, not just day seven. She quit therapy after the first session.

Threes work hard, and they can be excellent motivators of other people. John Bradshaw in the alcoholic treatment field and Jane Fonda in the aerobics teaching field are examples of Type Three personalties who are motivators in their respective fields.

Threes can also be very critical about those who don't work hard. A saying like "If you're not a solution to the problem, you are part of the problem." This is an expression of Type Three's attitude toward those who interfere with productivity.

TO BE EFFICIENT

Efficiency is necessary to produce at a competitive level. Threes are the people who have been labeled Type A personalities, heart attack prone individuals. They try to do more and more in less and less time. Eating, shaving, reading the newspaper and watching sports on television all at the same time is normal for a Three. "If you want to get something done, give it to a busy person," is a saying that refers to Type Threes. Threes are busy. But they are also efficient, can manage several tasks at the same time and are pragmatic. Threes get things done! They don't like to spend much of their time thinking. They like action and production. They know how to quickly turn their ideas into action.

Their schedules are always crammed and demanding. Threes make mental or written lists of what to do each day, week and year. They constantly prioritize and reprioritize their lists to be more efficient.

Threes are responsible when it comes to work and getting things done. "The buck stops here," is one of their mottos. Yet they are also excellent delegators and don't feel it is necessary for them to do everything personally. However, in spite of their capacity to delegate, they usually retain sufficient work for themselves to require long work days.

TO BE SOCIALLY ADMIRED

Threes want to be socially desirable and admired. As a result, they are usually socially sophisticated and relate to people easily. In fact, they are so capable of adjusting their personality to fit their environment that they have often been called chameleons. They cultivate a stereotypically male or female image. While most people don't notice the lack of depth behind their optimistic, happy and successful presentation, they may also be viewed as phony and superficial. What you see is all that is there. Prestige is very important. As one Type Three expressed, "Prestige makes me feel good, and it can open a lot of doors where I work."

You may get confused by their chameleon behavior and shallowness. They do too. They often don't know who the person is or even if one exists under the role they play to obtain the approval of society. These are the people who will try to have the picture-perfect family but remain unconcerned or unaware about the true health of their family. While they say they work hard for and often brag about their family, their spouse is often angry about the little time spent at home. And the children feel like their love and loyalty are being purchased with gifts, and that they are being pushed too hard to achieve. These are the people who come home from work one day to find the family has "split" and they are dumfounded. They thought everything at home was perfect. It was. But it was only "picture perfect."

Threes are the people seen in pictures in the social section of newspapers. They like being visible in a group and are sometimes labeled peacocks. Even if their occupation isn't in marketing, they market themselves continuously. When you're on the receiving end, their communication often feels more like propaganda. If you meet them at a party you will know their most flattering activities, accomplishments and goals within a few minutes. And you may hear a few exaggerated or completely fictitious stories about their achievements.

WINGS OF A THREE

When Threes lean to their Two Wing, they are more supportive and less competitive with their co-workers. They may be mentors to young people.

Achievers who lean toward their Four Wing tend to be moody and work in spurts. When they are up, they work extra hard and effectively. When they are down, they hide out and avoid people. They tend to enjoy being elite and unusual

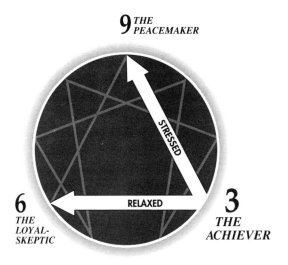

Stress and Relaxation

When **RELAXED** Threes move to the Six position on the Enneagram, their underlying fear of failure emerges. They become doubtful and suspicious about the motives of others, their competition. It's extremely difficult for Threes to relax.

When they do relax or even think about relaxation, they become doubtful about their own ability to achieve. They need to become productive to feel better again. It is easy to see why Threes have difficulty taking time off from work.

When Threes are **STRESSED** they move to the Nine position on the Enneagram. They become overwhelmed and try to numb their pain with sleep, drugs or daydreaming. They move from achieving to thoughts about achievement. Thoughts about achievement become a substitute for actual work. One Three reported that he would "space out" in his history class, a place he "hated to be" and think of all the money he'd make after college.

RECOGNIZING A REPRESENTATIVE THREE

Threes tend to talk fast, brag and try to sell you on their achievements and success. Their self-marketing is usually too "pat" and doesn't include mentioning any problems. They are always busy and have more to do than time to do it in. Arnold Schwarzenegger is representative of a Type Three who will do whatever it takes to be viewed as successful at whatever he does: body building, acting or marriage.

Their chameleon-like talent to become whatever they feel will make them appear successful in any environment and with any group of people is often amazing. Either they dress and act according to what is expected of them, or they are so obsessed with work and achievement that they don't pay any attention to how they dress and act around others. The tension which comes with overwork is usually seen in their face. They often live through and copy other Achievers. They idealize and talk about successful people such as sports figures, movie stars, and political leaders.

SUB-TYPES OF TYPE THREE

INTIMATE RELATIONSHIPS:
ROLE PLAYING

This sub-type takes on the appearance or plays the role of what they believe society expects the perfect man, woman, professional, marriage or family to be like. A very successful man I knew purchased horses for everyone in his family, even though no one in the family was really interested in horses. He talked about the horses extensively especially with business associates. For him, having horses was great – it was a great American family image and a symbol of success.

SOCIAL RELATIONSHIPS: PRESTIGE

Prestige sub-types are very concerned about being the best, being admired, and seeking praise from others. One Type Three described his social relationships this way; "I try to be the best and most admired in each group I am a part of. At work I may act one way with co-workers and differently with management to gain their admiration. With management I behave like the ideal employee. I act different with friends and family in order to be looked up to. I even dress, most of the time, the way I feel other people would like me to, with my own touch thrown into it." Prestige Threes are sometimes labeled chameleons.

They belong to the right club and seek to be invited to the right party. Belonging to the right club means prestige; whether or not they enjoy or value club activities is irrelevant.

SELF PRESERVATION: SECURITY

This sub-type seeks security based on the number and quality of the objects they possess. The function of the objects is secondary. They aren't secure in a comfortable house. It must be an expensive house in the "right" neighborhood with a prestigious address.

Clothes must not only be fashionable, but recognizably fashionable. The status label or monogram should be tastefully applied yet easily visible. They often dress their partners for success. One Three reported buying clothes for his dates to make sure they would make *him* look successful.

These are people who, if they buy a station wagon, must have a Mercedes wagon. Have you ever wondered why so many people have expensive boats in harbors but rarely use them? Many are Type Threes who have the boats for security and image.

One Type Three summed it up by saying, "I take pride in who I am and my accomplishments. Everything I am and have, I have done on my own. I have worked and sacrificed a lot, so I take pride in it. Since I am always working to climb the ladder of success at work, I also dress the part; my wardrobe consists of quality casual clothes and the best business attire. Everything is always to the 'T'."

Threes even objectify their relationships and find security in marrying a high-status or "quality" spouse who looks good, won't slow them down and will "facilitate" their pursuit of success.

THE ARTIST
TYPE FOUR

"Don't you wish you could be like me...My mood shifts seem to come from nowhere...My relationships are good for a while but never seem to work out...Dancing, art or the theater are my joys in life...I am too complicated for people to understand..." Fours are the most creative and theatrical of the Enneagram types. A Four's life is usually an internal melodrama that is sometimes shared with close friends. The drama includes yearning for loves lost and for extraordinary love in the future. It includes mood swings from feelings of elation and elitism to depression and self-rejection. For most Fours, sadness or depression is a frequent companion.

Fours are performers, dancers, writers, poets and artists – people like John Lennon and Orson Welles. They often stand out in a crowd due to their unusual and unique style of dress, or else they are not socially visible but at a subtle level appear unique. They detest the idea of being considered ordinary.

The **compelling desire** of Fours is to feel special, unique and privately elite. Preoccupation with romantic tragedies and avoiding being ordinary are ways to feel elite and to avoid underlying feelings (their deepest fear) of defectiveness and being emotionally overwhelmed.

ASSOCIATED DESIRES

The six associated desires of the Type Four personality are the desire to be privately elite, to consume, to be strong, to feel loved, to feel understood and to avoid depression.

Fours seem to be much more aware of the inner conflicts resulting from their desires than other Enneagram types. While on the one hand they want to be unique and elite, on the other hand they want to be accepted, which involves being ordinary. Although they want to be understood, if people do understand them they fear not feeling different or elite. They want to feel strong and yet be sensitive. They seem to dislike and at the same time revel in their mood swings.

PRIVATE ELITENESS

Fours are driven by the desire to be elite and are paradoxically often envious of the very people they see as being boring and ordinary. They constantly compare themselves with others and are often envious of others. They want to feel superior. But they feel the grass is always greener somewhere else or for someone else. Everyone else seems to be happier and has loving relationships. "I want to feel different on the outside, but I believe that somewhere on the inside I wish that I were like everyone else," remarked one Four.

They often are involved in one-on-one competition and are very envious. "My competition has to do with working to have men be attracted to me more than to my girlfriend," remarked one Type Four. There is a sense of arrogance about their own self-worth which helps to feed their competitive behavior. "Being envious makes me work harder to achieve," wrote another Type Four. Yet another Type Four reported, "I am very envious of other people, and I like to be the center of attention. No matter what the case may be, I like people to notice me. I go dancing a lot and was in a dance production to be better than others."

If you want to insult Fours, call them ordinary. In their attempts to be different and elite, they often appear to be eccentric or paradoxically extraordinarily natural. So while many Fours dress and style their hair in unusual and unique styles, others work to look natural. I knew one Four who used to spend hours putting on her makeup. When she was finished, she looked "natural," yet paradoxically, uniquely natural. Whatever they do, Fours do it creatively.

One Type Four had a very clever way of expressing his creativity and uniqueness. "I often wake up in the morning with messy hair. Sometimes, I carefully spray my hair with hairspray to maintain the messy hair look all day without having to comb it. I would then go to school with this outrageous hair, so that I could be different."

Paradoxically, one of the ways Fours try to be elite is to deny that they seek eliteness, even though in the privacy of their inner world they know how important feeling elite is to them. In my classes and workshops many Fours have denied that they try to be elite because they think I am referring to public eliteness (admiration) which is what some ordinary person might seek.

TO CONSUME

Some Type Fours and Type Twos are very impulsive. They are shop-'til-they-drop enthusiasts. Both Fours and Twos have difficulty setting limits for themselves and, as a result, can be very impulsive. One of the differences between the excessive shopping of Twos and Fours is that Twos tend to shop for others and to please others, whereas Fours tend to shop for themselves to "feel better."

The feelings of eliteness of the Type Four and the feelings of deservedness of the Privilege subtype of Type Two combine to produce compulsive spenders. Some Fours and Twos consider money to be something to "get rid of." I recall one Type Four who spent over fifty thousand dollars a year on clothes. It took her husband two years of pleading, nagging, threatening, cutting up credit cards, calling department stores and talking to therapists to reduce her spending. She was essentially incapable of and uninterested in setting her own limits on spending. Her consumption was fueled by her privileged attitude that "normal rules don't apply to me."

For some Fours, this compulsion to consume and "push the limits" can lead to shoplifting and petty theft. Such illegal activities are also fueled by Fours tendency to "live on the edge" and "make their own rules." It's by pushing things to their limits that Fours try to experience their boundaries and feel elite. Many Fours experience their eliteness internally and avoid direct public expressions of their eliteness. They also push limits in ways which aren't confrontive or public. "I don't pay traffic tickets, return books to the library, or pay for my auto license," remarked one Four.

Many Fours are competitive shoppers. If a friend buys something, they need it also. Their consumption must be unique. They will purchase clothes from the Goodwill thrift store or the most exclusive stores possible. They live in a funky house or in a high-status house. I remember one Four who couldn't afford to build the best house in an exclusive neighborhood, so he built the least expensive and most rustic house in the same exclusive neighborhood.

Fours like to be trendsetters and try to do things that "can't be done." They tend to break new ground, whether it's in what they chose to consume, participating in high risk activities such as bungee jumping, or in avant garde artistic expression.

TO BE STRONG

Fours are very vulnerable and sensitive. "At times I feel everyone can see right through me, and it's very unnerving." Fours tend to personalize the behavior of other people, leading them to feel ashamed and socially inferior. Their sensitivity to the feelings of other people is so deep that they often feel other people's pain, and they frequently have difficulty discerning whether or not the pain they're experiencing is theirs or another person's. Their sensitivity makes them more understanding about the feelings of others. Because of their thin psychological boundaries, they are self-revealing to significant others. They frequently regret their tendency to be overly open in the expression of their emotions.

Because of their vulnerable and sensitive nature, they often seek strength through someone else who has strong boundaries and is in control. One Type Four expressed how she was strengthened by and yet could feel free in a relationship with a Type Eight personality, the Controller. The Type Eight personality set definitive limits on her behavior. However, she was able to be free and "do her own thing" within those limits.

Even though Type Fours, like Type Eights, don't feel that the rules of society apply to them, they don't generally break the law. Instead, they will push the law to its limits, and find clever ways to, in effect, break the law while living within the limits of the law. For example, one Type Four reported that he printed and distributed an "underground newspaper" in high school. The school authorities didn't like it, but he went about it in a way which didn't technically violate any of the school's policies. His attitude was "I don't break the rules. I circumvent them."

To Feel Loved

Groucho Marx expressed the difficulty Fours have in relating well to others when he said, "I would never belong to a club that would have me as a member."

Developing interpersonal relationships is the focal point of their lives. They are love addicts. They hope for and dream about meeting an ideal mate. In the meantime, they focus on what's missing in the current relationship. Intimate relationships with Fours are very difficult. They tend to dwell on sweet memories of past relationships and hopes for the future. "I almost always dwell on my last relationship, even if I was the one to break up the relationship. I dwell on these 'sweet' memories until I am involved in another relationship."

When they do achieve an intimate relationship, Fours never really feel loved, and they expect their mates to prove their love over and over again. Despite constant reassurance, they find ways to discount every attempt made by others to make them feel loved. In spite of these loving gestures and constant reassurance, they still feel something is missing. Their fear of abandonment and their fear that at any moment something may destroy the relationship is more intense than for the Type Two personality.

To avoid abandonment, Fours will often abandon the other person first. One Type Four reported, "At one time, I used to leave loving relationships when the man I was with committed to marriage. I think that my fears of a tragic abandonment became too intense. I left him to prevent him from eventually leaving me."

Fours will continually test your love for them - by overspending, by demanding time and by expecting you to always place them first in your life. The message is "If you **really** loved me you would ..." Rarely can their mate pass the test. And if they should happen to pass it, a new test will soon be administered.

Relationships with Fours are like being on a roller coaster by the intensity of their mood swings. And they can't contain or hide their emotions well when they are with people who are close to them. Such emotional volatility is often more visible at home than in the office and in other public places.

TO FEEL UNDERSTOOD

At one level, their feelings of eliteness are fed by their pride in believing that other people don't and can't understand them. One Type Four said, "I'm above the masses. They will never be able to understand me." At a deeper level, Fours wish people could understand them.

Fours often suffer from intense mood swings. Periods of depression, where they experience very deep and often dark sides of their psyches, which alternate with intense highs that bring them in contact with excitement, optimism and joy. Fours don't think other people feel these extremes and therefore can't understand them. And, in a way, they are right - other personality types don't generally experience these extremes. However, similar feelings are buried deep in the unconscious of each of us. That's one reason why we are drawn to the extremes often revealed in the creative expressions of artists. The melancholy expressed in the poetry, art or stories of the Type Four touches a deep place within ourselves.

Some Fours have an unusual capacity to understand others through their creative expressions. One Type Four who is an artist said that she could "feel the emotional expression of other artists" by immersing herself psychologically in their artwork.

Even though Fours long to be understood, they feel it is virtually impossible for others to understand them unless it's through some form of symbolic expression such as art, poetry or writing. Their intense desire to express themselves artistically is an expression of their frustration due to feeling misunderstood, an attempt to better understand themselves and a desire to share that understanding with others.

Paradoxically, they seem to take some pride in the idea that no one can understand them. One Type Four said, with a look and a voice expressing pride, "No one can understand me except another Type Four."

TO AVOID DEPRESSION

Fours never really seem at home in moment-to-moment contact with their deepest feelings. Because they unconsciously strive to avoid their underlying feelings of depression and defectiveness, they live in the future or in the past. Their fantasies, daydreams, and dramatizations help them avoid making sustained contact with a "present moment" feeling. Rarely do they feel relaxed, comfortable and in harmony with the world. For most Fours, the present moment is filled with despair, self-rejection or sweet regret.

Mood changes for most Type Fours are impossible to avoid. Moods seem to "sweep in" and to "take charge" of them. Sometimes Fours feel secure, elite and superior, and at other times they feel insecure, not wanted, angry and/or depressed. Such mood swings can cause them to want to be overly sociable or painfully reclusive. As one Four reported, "At times I feel very social, like a 'social butterfly,' the absolute center of attention. At other times I may want nothing more than to be completely alone, separate even from the one I love."

Such mood swings seem like an unconscious attempt to avoid facing the intensity of their undesirable feelings in the present. Somewhat like a pendulum swings from one extreme to the other with only a dash through the equilibrium point, Fours tend to swing from highs to lows without passing through the present moment. They don't want to face the underlying, nagging feeling that something is wrong or defective with them.

When Fours are depressed, it can be a deep, black depression, triggering a depressive and/or angry withdrawal from the world or a high intensity of activity to avoid painful or negative feelings. They enjoy the excitement of risk-taking and the intense feelings which risk-taking can generate in order to distract them from the feelings of suffering which exist in the present.

Even though the mood swings are a central issue for Fours, they are at one level desirous of the mood swings. They believe the swings make them unique and add depth to their being. One Type Four observed that the personality types he would least like to be were Types Nine and Five because their moods were too steady. He felt this would lead to a boring and "middle of the road" life. However another Four married a Type Nine because he was "smart, reliable and most of all, stable."

WINGS OF A FOUR

Shirley MacLaine is an example of a Type Four who leans toward her Three Wing. In addition to being creative, she is enterprising, productive and achievement oriented.

Fours, who lean toward their Five Wing, are more likely to express their creativity in cerebral pursuits such as writing books or music.

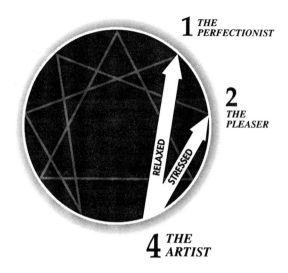

1 **THE**
   PERFECTIONIST

2
THE
PLEASER

4 **THE**
   ARTIST

STRESS AND RELAXATION

When Fours are **STRESSED** they move to the Two Point. They feel an intense need for love, and they become very giving and helpful. "When the Two in me comes to life, I am able to please and help my boyfriend before he even asks me to." Another Four reported, "When I am stressed I cook, clean and shop for others more than myself." The stress that shifts them to the Two Point is often real or imagined rejection.

When Fours are **RELAXED** their inner critic emerges. They move to the One Point and become perfectionistic and critical. A Type Four who is an artist reported that the relaxed feelings which she experienced when she finished preparing for an art exhibition also triggered a critical appraisal of her work and a drive to perfect her paintings even more. The combination of the creativity, desire to do what "can't be done" and the search for perfection when relaxed helps to explain the extraordinary artistic talent of Type Fours.

It's easy to see why Fours often have difficulty establishing smooth relationships. When they are stressed, they are Pleasers (Type Two). They will do anything for you, and you can do no wrong. However, when they are relaxed they are Perfectionists

(Type One). They compare you to their "daydream fantasy," the perfect person and they become very critical of you and "expect" improvement.

RECOGNIZING A REPRESENTATIVE TYPE FOUR

Many Fours have a look of sadness or cloudiness in their eyes, reflecting their feelings of melancholy. Their clothes and general appearance are usually unique and different or else understated and very ordinary. If you are perceptive, you can see a subtle arrogance. Their communication style conveys an underlying feeling of regret and sadness. They talk about tragedies of the past in a sad and often forlorn tone of voice. They avoid "small talk" because that is for ordinary people. Their feelings of eliteness are often experienced by others as arrogance and vanity. When they aren't "down," they usually want to be with you. When they are down, they tend to seek isolation.

SUB-TYPES OF TYPE FOUR

Type Four sub-types focus on avoiding feelings of rejection and depression.

INTIMATE RELATIONSHIPS: COMPETITION

Intimate Fours are competitive in all their relationships, especially intimate relationships. They want to feel valued by their mate as special, their one and only love. "I wanted to be my mate's first love, and I'm always envious of his first real love because I think she must have been loved more by him."

SOCIAL RELATIONSHIPS:
SHAME

Social Fours have an inner conflict about group situations. They want to relate socially, but they feel ashamed in social situations. They feel that other people will see them and reject them because of their "inner defectiveness."

SELF-PRESERVATION:
RECKLESS

Self-Preservation Fours live on the edge. They are high-energy people who are willing to risk everything to succeed at their creative endeavor. They push their limits and will often indulge in what appears to others as reckless behavior such as speeding on a motorcycle or sky diving.

CHAPTER

7

PEOPLE OF THE HEAD

THE HEAD CENTER
TYPES FIVE, SIX AND SEVEN

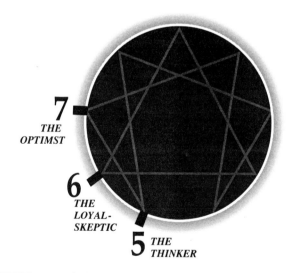

7
THE
OPTIMST

6
THE
LOYAL-
SKEPTIC

5 *THE*
THINKER

Types Five, Six, and Seven are associated with the *head center.* They are primarily motivated by the avoidance of fear, and they retreat into their head to avoid experiencing emotions which are painful or fearful. Fives think to avoid the uncertainty and anxiety which can accompany most emotional experiences. Sixes worry and over-prepare intellectually in an attempt to avoid the anxiety that arises from the unpredictability and threatening intentions they suspect underlie the behavior of other people. Sevens think optimistically and are always planning new things to do as a way to stay in their head and thus avoid anything more than brief contact with potentially painful emotions.

THE THINKER
TYPE FIVE

"Did you know that...My collection is unmatched...I enjoy being alone...Emotions interfere with thinking...Hmmm, let me have more time to think about it...Give me space to think...It's fascinating to watch people..." Five is the home of the expert, the scholar, the recluse and the collector of the unusual. They are the philosopher, rare art collector and the scientist.

The **compelling desire** of thinkers is to learn, analyze and collect unusual knowledge. Thinking keeps them distant from the dark side which is their emotions. Thinking keeps them in their head, away from the emotionally alive central portion of their body and thereby limits their emotional life. Unconsciously they are afraid that they will either be overwhelmed by their emotions or find only emptiness if they do attempt to sense the central part of their body and become aware of their emotions.

ASSOCIATED DESIRES

The associated desires of the Type Five personality are to become an expert, to cling to their possessions, to detach socially, to detach emotionally, and to limit their life.

TO BECOME AN EXPERT

Just as Type Twos can never get enough love to satisfy them, Type Fives can never learn enough. They enjoy learning in general and often pursue professions such as a computer programmer or physicist. They don't just want any knowledge, they want special, quantifiable knowledge about something other people don't know very much about. They often become expert in detailed and sometimes obscure areas of knowledge. Richard Feynman, a Nobel Prize-winning physicist, was a Type Five personality whose eyes gleamed with excitement when he talked about theoretical physics or some rare culture he was investigating.

One of my clients refers to a friend of his, a Type Five personality, as a "master of the absurd." This friend constantly shares unusual and "off the wall" facts such as what Elvis Presley would eat for breakfast or President Bush's golf score.

Often the expertise of a Type Five shifts from knowing about some rare or special topic to actually collecting items. They become collectors of old toy trucks, confetti, swizzle sticks or some other rare or special item.

At a football game, a Type Three is concerned with which team is winning and the strategy for winning. A Type Five personality would be more interested in the statistics of the game than they would be in who wins or loses the game.

To Cling To Possessions

Type Fives hold onto things in an effort to make their life simple and manageable. They cling to and are stingy with their money and time as well as their emotions. Even their thoughts are sparingly shared. One Type Five jokingly said that when he attempts to discard any of his possessions, they usually end up littering the floor of his room rather than finding their way to the garbage can. Another Five labeled herself a "pack rat."

To Detach Socially

At social gatherings, Fives tend to stand back and observe other people from a distance. They are very judgmental in their analysis of people and themselves. They are introverts, are very independent and have a strong need for privacy. They are the opposite of the socially sophisticated Threes. Fives consider most people to be not very bright and mostly boring. They are very private people who enjoy spending a lot of time alone.

Fives might be called wallflowers because they literally disappear or are difficult to observe at social gatherings. Some accomplished and admired Fives have even perfected a way of not being seen while they are in the midst of a social gathering in their honor. They especially don't like interactions which focus attention on them.

They need to get to know someone well before they begin to risk opening up and becoming more intimate. When they do begin to trust you, their form of intimacy is usually sharing secret information rather than secret feelings. I know a Type Five, a spiritual teacher, whose primary way of being intimate with others is by sharing her spiritual knowledge rather than knowledge about her personal life.

TO DETACH EMOTIONALLY

Fives believe that emotions interfere with their ability to think objectively. The word love is generally unspoken. Emotions are considered to be unimportant. Only if they begin to feel too isolated and lonely will they become more open to their emotional life.

I remember a Type Five client who was in her early twenties and had never dated or had close friends. Her need for privacy, which she enjoyed for most of her life, had turned into loneliness. She was attractive, intelligent and wanted a boyfriend. Her primary issue upon entering therapy had been overwhelming anxiety. After about one year of psychotherapy, she rarely experienced overwhelming anxiety. However, when I would help her direct her attention to her stomach, pelvis or chest, where emotional feelings are located, she experienced difficulty feeling anything. When she was finally able to begin feeling in these areas, she reported feeling a "big empty void" which frightened and confused her.

I explained to her that one of the main reasons she didn't have any friends was not due to lack of social skills or attractiveness, but because she was, at an unconscious level, afraid that intimate feelings might stir up her unconscious feelings of emptiness. The focus of the therapy was shifted to helping her "enter" the emptiness psychologically, and to help her slowly discover and become more comfortable with her feelings. We talked very little about relationships. However, as she bravely and slowly made more and more contact with her own feelings, she began to develop intimate relationships with other people.

In another instance, I recall remarking to a self-identified Five how amazed I was that he was so emotionally alive and could make such good eye contact. He said, "It took practice. My eye contact and my out-going personality are an act. I wasn't really looking into your eyes. I was looking at your eyebrows. I was only pretending to be emotionally available."

Fives will often think far into the future to limit potential future emotional arousal. For example, one Type Five said that he thinks a lot about the possible death of important people in his life, even when there is no reason to expect them to die. He felt that he could limit his emotional reaction to someone's death in the future if he prepared himself enough by thinking about it now. Another way he reported coping with thoughts of death was to consider death to be simply "another state of mind."

TO LIMIT THEIR LIFE

Fives tend to limit their lives not only socially and emotionally but also by living in a small space with limited possessions. Limiting the physical space in which they live is consistent with how they limit themselves to their head as a limited home in their body. It is an attempt to make both their internal and external life safe and manageable.

Their living space is usually small and efficiently functional. If they are living with someone else, they will have a private room for an escape. They are proud that they can live in a small place and don't need many material comforts. I once visited a world-renowned nuclear scientist and was surprised at the small cluttered office that he occupied. His administrative assistant, a Type Three personality, had a large well-decorated office. I understand now that the scientist was a Type Five personality and had an office which fit his personality.

Whereas Threes often act without thinking, Fives will often think without ever acting. Like Ones, they have a strong and critical superego which causes them to be self-critical and to procrastinate. The Type One procrastinates because of their effort to be right. The Type Five procrastinates because they want more precise and detailed information.

WINGS OF A FIVE

Fives leaning toward their Six Wing have two reasons to avoid people. They are suspicious about the intentions of others and concerned that they will invade their space and interfere with their thinking.

Fives leaning toward their Four Wing may experience some of the Fours' tendency to prize being different. And, due to the elite characteristic of the Type Fours, these Fives may become even more disdainful of people who don't think deeply and originally. Also, leaning toward their Four Wing may mean their thinking will become more creative.

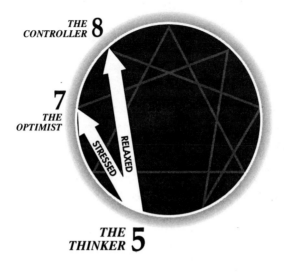

STRESS AND RELAXATION

When **STRESSED** Fives move to the Seven Point. They think about plans for future activities, and accomplishments related to their specialty. For example, they may intensify their efforts to add to their specialized collection of African pots.

Fives are one of the least conformist and difficult to control types on the Enneagram because they are the most out of touch with their feelings. They are quite certain that their opinions on life are well thought through and "unassailable."

When they are **RELAXED** their defenses are lowered and feelings begin to emerge. They move to the Eight Point to gain control and protect their emerging feelings of vulnerability. They become more militant and expressive about their nonconformist ways. And they resist control by others and actually try to control others by using their "I know better," aggressive and sarcastic posture.

RECOGNIZING A TYPE FIVE

Fives generally appear emotionally cool and detached and seem to stay on the fringe of groups. Their eyes have a subtle barrier quality which seems to block access to their inner life. Their conversational style is deliberate, exact and emotionless. When they explain things to you, they tend to do it in a slow, sequential, step-by-step way which may make you feel patronized or dumb. They don't think their physical appearance is important and as a result usually dress plainly. If they do try to relate to you, it will be by communicating important information, or if they really like you, secret information, as opposed to feelings.

SUB-TYPES OF A TYPE FIVE

INTIMATE RELATIONSHIPS:
CONFIDENTIALITY

Expressing love is not very important to Fives. Love is "not critical" to life, expressed one Five. And, "You don't have to express your love to anyone."

For Intimate Fives, sharing inside, special or confidential information is the foundation for coming close to someone in a private one-to-one interaction. For a mathematician, it can be sharing a "secret" mathematical formula or some mathematical "trick" which speeds up the problem-solving process.

SOCIAL RELATIONSHIPS:
SOURCE OF KNOWLEDGE

Social Fives connect in groups by either providing specialized information or by learning from some leader who is a source of specialized knowledge such as scientific information or esoteric spiritual wisdom. They like to tell you how to do things better or quicker. One Type Five related that he takes great pleasure in sharing his specialized knowledge about photography with other people.

SELF PRESERVATION:
WITHDRAWAL

Withdrawing into their own space provides Fives with a retreat where they can feel safe and secure. The space they withdraw into can be a room at home, a special place in the forest or camper at the beach. The important aspect of this space is that it is "their" special space and they have control over it. No one can invade it, and therefore they feel safe from emotional arousal and free to think.

THE LOYAL-SKEPTIC TYPE SIX

"I'm worried about...I am not sure what people think of me...Teamwork feels good to me...I like strong, trustworthy leaders...I won't do well...What do you mean by that...Be careful about what you say and do...Stay within the guidelines...Don't try new things...It seems like I never have enough information to make a good decision..." These statements reveal the Sixes' suspicion about the lack of predictability and fairness of their environment. They like well-led, predictable and organized groups.

Sixes are the dutiful policemen, firemen, and members of the armed forces whose work requirements and leadership expectations are well-defined. Counterphobic Sixes seek high-risk occupations such as stuntman or race car driver, actually seeking out the very dangers that they fear. Richard Nixon exemplifies the suspiciousness of the Type Six. Colonel Oliver North exemplifies Type Six Loyalty.

The **compelling drive** for Sixes is to feel secure. They are doubtful, careful, cautious and watchful. Predictability in jobs and relationships is sought in order to avoid anxiety. Anxiety, their dark side, is a product of uncertainty and underlies insecurity.

ASSOCIATED DESIRES

The associated desires for Type Sixes are the desire to achieve certainty, to enjoy predictability in relationships, to avoid threats from others, to be liked and to be free from persecution.

ACHIEVING CERTAINTY

The need for certainty is driven by doubt and anxiety. Sixes doubt many things about their internal life and their surrounding environment. They are the most likely participants in an Enneagram workshop to be uncertain about what type they really are and to doubt the suggestions of other people that they are a Type Six.

This desire to be certain causes them to procrastinate and to start and stop tasks repeatedly. Action involves change which leads to uncertainty and frequently anxiety. Sixes try to predict what will happen in the future but, because predicting the future is virtually impossible, Sixes often avoid trying anything new in an attempt to feel secure and certain.

Certainty is based on lack of doubt, which ultimately is related to trust. The mind can never feel certain. Logical arguments can never convince the mind to trust and be at peace. Trust leading to peace of mind is an aspect of essence. Releasing aspects of essence is introduced in Part Three of this book.

Feelings of uncertainty are also based on insecurity and weakness. Sixes unconsciously avoid feelings in the gut, which is where essential strength is concentrated. In general, it is difficult for Sixes to even attempt to experience feelings in the gut or belly area of the body, because anxiety and fear dominate that part of their body, where their essential strength is blocked. However, it is necessary to be aware of and stay aware of the feelings of weakness in the belly area before essential strength can emerge. For example, I was supporting a client's therapy efforts to make contact with essential strength in her belly. At first, it was difficult for her to feel any sensations there. Then she experienced a queasy, sick feeling in her belly. When her essential strength first began to emerge, she became very frightened, even though she reported feeling stronger, more relaxed and less doubtful.

Being rigid is another way in which Sixes seek certainty. They maintain a rigid allegiance to their ideals and belief system as well as to their established behaviors. They won't deviate from their position and will doggedly and angrily defend it.

Ones are also rigid, but for them the rigidity evolves from their inner critic, whereas Sixes are rigid in order to decrease uncertainty and to feel more secure.

NEEDING PREDICTABILITY

Sixes' need for certainty is idealized as "I am loyal." Sixes are team members. They seek jobs in organizations where people operate on the basis of clearly defined rules and lines of authority. Whether the team is their family or a company, they are proud of their loyalty. They work hard for the team and do what they are supposed to do. For example, I know one Type Six who never missed a day of work for over thirty years! He was especially proud that he came to work even when he was very ill.

Even though Sixes are very loyal, they view authority figures in general as incompetent. Although they complain relentlessly about their leaders, they rarely try to change the leadership because their certainty and security in the organization could be threatened. They complain about their job and the leadership, but rarely leave. On the other hand, if they feel betrayed by the leadership, they feel fully justified in changing their intense loyalty into intense betrayal. One employee I knew was fiercely loyal to his company until he was passed over for promotion for clearly political reasons. He became a severe critic of his boss and, without confronting his boss, did everything possible to undermine him.

This need for authority and the need to complain about authority creates ambivalent feelings about authority. Ambivalence is part of what keeps Sixes immobile, scared and procrastinating.

TO AVOID THREATS FROM OTHERS

Sixes doubt and mistrust their own intentions, so it is only reasonable that they would doubt, mistrust and be hyperalert to the intentions of others. They project some of their self-doubts onto other people. "I always try to second-guess the thoughts and motives of other people," wrote one Six. They are very mistrustful about the intentions of other people and are afraid people will treat them unfairly.

Sixes often identify with underdogs and are often helpful to those who are helpless. Their motive is not to be liked but to express their empathy with people who are helpless and who have been treated unfairly. It comforts them to feel that they themselves might be helped should they fail and become helpless.

Imagine being lost, late at night, in a run-down poorly lit section of a large city. Most of the people you pass are shabbily dressed, and all seem strange, weird or mean-looking. What will happen next? Will you be robbed? Will you be beaten up? Feel the anxiety and fear building inside you as you take this imaginary walk and notice how vigilant you become about everyone and everything in your environment. Is that person coming down the street a friend or foe? Along the way someone notices your disorientation and stops to see if you need help or to give you directions on how to get out of this part of town. "Is this person going to help me or lead me astray into a dangerous or life-threatening situation?" Imagine the feelings you would experience in this frightening environment for they are probably very similar to the feelings experienced in the day-to-day life of a Type Six personality.

This mistrust of other people can be seen more subtly in their inability to receive compliments easily. "I want people to compliment me, but as soon as they do, I feel weird," reported one Six. They are always looking for hidden messages, meanings or implications. So, if you compliment them on a job well done, they wonder, "What did he really mean?" "Will they expect more from me now?" If you want a Six to feel comfortable with your compliment, you may need to soften the compliment and make it appear more realistic by adding a negative qualifier. "You did an excellent job. **However,** you could have paid a little more attention to detail."

When confronted with well-defined, clear threats, the Six often becomes the hero. The heroism can be seen on the battlefield, in fighting fires, on the police force, or in professional athletics. President Bush is a Type Six, loyal and reliable. Before the Gulf War, many people considered President Bush to be a weak leader. At the time of the Gulf War many critics believed that even though he was a weak leader, he responded to the well-defined threat of Saddam Hussein by exhibiting strong leadership and decisiveness.

TO BE LIKED

Sixes please and want to be liked to feel secure. Their suspiciousness about others leads them to try to protect themselves by being ingratiating. Although their niceness may appear similar to that of a Type Two, their motivation is different because Twos please to avoid abandonment.

Sixes want to be respected as well as liked. They respect people who are strong and capable, and they want people to see them as similarly strong and capable.

TO BE FREE FROM CRITICISM

Sixes often feel harassed and annoyed by their own critical thoughts pertaining to themselves and what they fear everyone in the world may think about them. Paradoxically, they are often the greatest critics of other people. They are hyperalert and sensitive to the intentions of other people as a way to keep one step in front of their criticism. Sixes long to be accepted and judged as competent.

WINGS OF A SIX

The Wings of a Six are Types Five and Seven. When Sixes lean in the Seven direction, they constantly stay in their head thinking and coping with uncertainty about their plans for the future and the fun things they could do in life. The apparently carefree life of the Seven is very appealing to Sixes.

Sixes leaning toward the Five Point tend to rationalize their feelings of insecurity and to seek more certainty in life by developing a comforting philosophy of life.

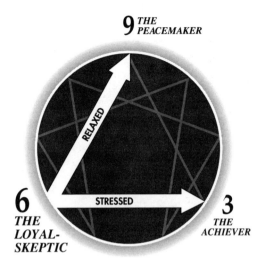

STRESS AND RELAXATION

When **STRESSED** the Six moves to the Three Point which results in their striving to be more successful by accomplishing more. It is as if, when they are stressed, they become even more fearful of "not making it" and seek to be more productive and thus achieve greater security. But the added work often produces more stress and insecurity.

On the other hand, many Sixes want to be Threes because their achievements as Threes would make them admirable and lead to less criticism from others. And, in spite of their self-doubt, they become very productive. They sometimes burn-out from a combination of too much work and too much worry.

When **RELAXED** the Six moves to the Nine Point. Their defenses soften, and they tend to become lethargic and numb. These deadened, lethargic feelings feel good to the Six because they narcoticize their anxiety to some extent. One Six reported, "I like to feel numb, I don't worry so much then."

RECOGNIZING A SIX TYPE

Their communication is cautious and tentative. They subtly seek agreement from other people while stating their own position. An ingratiating smile is used by Sixes more frequently than other types to disarm potential threats. You may have noticed how you tend to smile more when trying to communicate with someone who speaks a different language or in a foreign country where you feel insecure. The hesitant smile, the slight look of fear and anxiety in the eyes - these are the hallmarks of interaction with a Type Six.

SUB-TYPES OF A TYPE SIX

These sub-types focus on achieving security in an unpredictable, untrustworthy world.

INTIMATE RELATIONSHIPS:
STRENGTH AND BEAUTY

The Intimate Six is often counter-phobic, moving toward the very danger which they fear. Intimate Sixes display strength even though they feel insecure. They are usually attractive and are attracted to other strong and attractive people. Stuntmen, mountain climbers and similar high-risk activities include many Intimate Sixes in their ranks. Evel Kneivel is probably an Intimate Six.

Intimate Sixes may be confused with Eights or Threes, who appear similarly powerful - it's the underlying motivation which differentiates them. The Six displays power to counter fear of uncertainty, the Eight to gain control and the Three to be admired.

SOCIAL RELATIONSHIPS:
DUTIFUL

Dutiful Sixes are especially dedicated to their family, friends and employers. They are the clean-cut Marine, Police Officer or

Fireman. They are the dedicated spouse and parent.

Their dedication extends to their parents long after leaving home. The Dutiful Six is compelled to do what their parents expect regardless of their own feelings. This creates a love-hate relationship causing frequent fights and conflicts.

SELF-PRESERVATION:
WARMTH

Sixes are warm, caring, people-pleasers, much like Twos. The difference is their underlying motivation. Twos please to avoid abandonment. Sixes are warm and caring to disarm a perceived threat and to feel secure. Warm Sixes exhibit an anxiousness, which differentiates them from the calmer Type Twos.

THE OPTIMIST TYPE SEVEN

"I had the most fun...He was the funniest person...Let's plan to go somewhere together...I'll clean the car tomorrow...I generally trust people...Things always work out for the best..." Sevens are generally charming, uplifting and fun to be around. They want everyone to be optimistic and happy. They like a good time and are always planning their next adventure. They are the writers, planners, advertisers, idealists, flight attendants and nutritional instructors. Their motto is, "Don't worry, be happy."

Magic Johnson exemplifies the Type Seven personality. His bright eyes, big smile and uplifting attitude are notorious. Even after discovering that he was infected with the HIV virus, he remained happy and lighthearted. He immediately became involved in a flurry of plans and activities to promote AIDS awareness, purchased a professional basketball franchise, helped the Laker basketball team and competed in the Olympics. People wondered how he could remain so positive. If you understand the Enneagram, you realize that, just like the scorpion discussed in Chapter One, Magic has no choice. His personality type compels him to be optimistic and have multiple plans, especially when he is faced with emotional pain. Barbara Streisand is another noteworthy Seven.

The **compelling desire** of a Type Seven is to have fun, keep busy with activities and future plans and be optimistic. Out of fear, they avoid painful emotions, boredom and facing life's difficulties which may emerge if they let their planning and optimism subside.

ASSOCIATED DESIRES

The associated desires for a Type Seven are the desire to keep things light, uplift others, have fun, plan for future fun and never miss out.

KEEP THINGS LIGHT

Think happy thoughts, have an optimistic outlook and everything will work out for the best. Just don't bring me down. Don't force me to face painful aspects of life. "I know everything will be all right. I can do anything." These statements reflect the Sevens' efforts to keep things light.

If you want to discuss some serious but painful issue with a Seven, you will find it very difficult to get them to slow down enough to talk. The solution is to tell them that you need to talk to them and, as funny as it may seem, make an appointment. Of course, if you have something funny or interesting to talk to them about, Sevens always have (make) time.

Their idealism and optimism help them avoid painful aspects of life. To other people they often seem overly optimistic and superficial. One Seven wrote, "Living more on the light and sunny side of life brought accusations from some people that I was somewhat superficial. They don't seem to think that I'm a person of substance and meaning." More severe accusations are that they are phony. They usually brush off these accusations by rationalizations or an abrupt change of topic.

The Sevens' optimistic and idealistic world view is not to be tampered with. If someone persists in challenging their "light" lifestyle, they can become explosive in their own defense and be severely critical of the person challenging their optimism. Don't mess with their view of reality or their schedules and plans.

It may take severe "blows from reality" to cause Sevens to wake up to some of the difficult realities that are a necessary part of a healthy life, like sticking to commitments, facing and resolving conflict, being self-disciplined and accepting responsibilities.

Their optimistic attitude extends to how they view other people. "I tend to see the good side of people." The good news is that they make friends easily. The bad news is that they aren't as aware of people who can take advantage of them because they are excessively trusting. They are frequently the victims of con artists.

UPLIFT OTHERS

When a smiling, lighthearted, and fun-loving Seven enters a room, people are uplifted. Sevens like to laugh and cheer people up. Being playful, cute and jovial enlivens those around them.

When they encounter someone who is depressed or feeling low, they feel, as one Seven put it, that "It is my duty to lift their spirits, to help them forget about their woes. Few can uplift people as well as I can!"

To keep their own energy up and create an uplifting environment for themselves, Sevens have a broad and diverse group of friends. They enjoy being with unique and unusual combinations of people. Surprising friends with gifts or special parties is exciting and uplifting for many Sevens.

HAVE FUN

Having fun is a way for Sevens to escape pain and drudgery. "I have always tried to see the brighter, more optimistic side of every dreary situation, no matter how bleak. I am always thinking of new ways to have fun, new places to visit, anything that seems interesting or can offer an escape from the everyday drudgeries of life."

Humor is an important way Sevens enjoy life. "I find humor in nearly every situation, which makes life altogether enjoyable. I also find humor in nearly all people that I meet. Even if a person isn't trying to be funny, something they say or do will make me laugh."

The rebelliousness of Sevens is related to their need to be free to have fun, keep their options open and avoid life's difficulties. They can be hot-headed and angry if you try to interfere with or don't support their plans for fun.

PLAN FOR FUTURE FUN

Planning and doing enjoyable activities are the trademarks of a Seven. Even while they are participating in the current enjoyable activity, they are planning the next trip, party, date or career move.

Planning for future fun, living in dreams of future enjoyment and being constantly active can lead to a lack of discipline and make it difficult for Sevens to follow through on important responsibilities. "I basically fill every minute of my day with activity. If I don't, I feel this uneasiness that ultimately propels me into some sort of activity. I want to experience all that there is to experience. I can remember my mother asking me if I felt life was a three-ring circus, and did I think that it was necessary for me to perform in all three rings. My answer was yes!"

Their active mind and optimistic attitude makes them creative. Imagining new ideas is natural to them. Unusual parties or activities are a part of their lifestyle.

NEVER MISS OUT

Keeping busy, their options open and commitments light, gives them the feeling that they won't miss out on the fun. One Seven wrote, "I overindulge out of a fear of being deprived of what I want. This fear is to a great extent what governs my behavior. And I encourage others to 'go for it' too."

During a class discussion about death, a Seven shared that he often had strong fears about dying. I had difficulty not smiling when he shared the circumstances surrounding his fear of death. His intense fear of death occurs during the day of a big party. He is afraid he will die that day and not get to go to the party.

Moving from job to job and relationship to relationship helps to keep things light and ensures that they won't miss out on anything in life. Many Sevens are virtually unable to make a commitment to just one job or one relationship.

They are sought after as friends and companions because they are so enjoyable to be around. And they like to have a lot of friends. If they can't get you to like them by uplifting you, they may seduce you in a childlike, pleasing way, with the objective of wanting you to like them and making them feel good. When they are liked, they have more friends and are less likely to miss out on all that life has to offer. And being around their group of friends **is** a party.

WINGS OF A SEVEN

Sevens who lean toward the Eight Wing have a tougher appearance, are more argumentative and need to have control of their own life. When Sevens lean toward their Six Wing, they tend to be less optimistic and more suspicious about people.

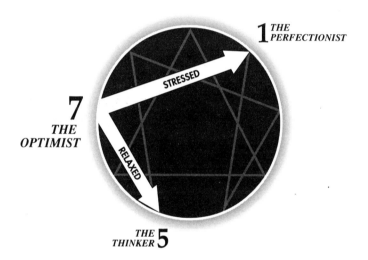

STRESS AND RELAXATION

When **STRESSED** Sevens become critical and judgmental, like Type Ones. Stress for Sevens often occurs when someone is interfering with their plans for fun. Their defense against pain, which is having fun and planning for fun, is threatened. Their lighthearted ways can quickly change to anger and criticism.

When Sevens are **RELAXED** they move to Point Five on the Enneagram. Relaxed, they slow down somewhat and can focus their attention and think more clearly. Even when relaxed, they don't want to think about reducing their level of activities. They often use the thinking which is associated with Type Five personalities to intensify their planning and to justify and rationalize their fun-seeking behavior.

RECOGNIZING A TYPE SEVEN

Seven's conversations are filled with entertaining, self-gratifying and funny stories about their personal experiences. They are bright-eyed and usually have a smile on their face. Their childlike energy and enthusiasm are infectious. They are always on the move unless they are very tired. They will try to uplift you and share their excitement about their fun-filled plans for the future.

SUB-TYPES OF A TYPE SEVEN

INTIMATE RELATIONSHIPS: POSITIVE IMAGINATION

Intimate Sevens have short attention spans and are always seeking new and different experiences in life. They don't stay in relationships long. Their motto is "Don't tie me down." One of the ways to become intimate with this sub-type is to share plans and options.

SOCIAL RELATIONSHIPS: SACRIFICE

These Sevens feel dutiful or loyal to their family and job. They "stuff" their longings for change and adventure and think that they must put the family, job or spouse first. They often feel like martyrs and harbor deep resentments about their commitments.

SELF-PRESERVATION:
GROUP SECURITY

Self-preservation Sevens need to feel a part of a close-knit group beyond their family. They often consider this group to be an extended family which is often more important than their own family. "I have a group of friends whom I've known since high school. We stand by each other, share our hopes and dreams. We're like a family."

8

PEOPLE OF THE GUT

THE GUT CENTER
TYPES EIGHT, NINE AND ONE

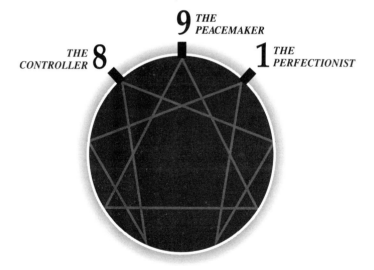

9 *THE PEACEMAKER*

THE CONTROLLER 8

1 *THE PERFECTIONIST*

Types Eight, Nine and One are associated with the *gut center*. The central underlying issue for the gut center is anger. They control themselves and resist being controlled by other people.

Eights are the most defiant and won't let anyone control them. They *express* anger openly and directly. At a deep level they feel justified in their expression of anger because of injustices they experienced in childhood. Their anger may be expressed by being confrontive, controlling themselves and others, or by getting back at people who "wrong them." Eights use these expressions of anger to protect themselves from feeling weak or vulnerable to potentially unjust treatment by other people.

Eights feel more powerful than the other personality types. Their control of self and others keeps them from feeling weak and vulnerable. Intimacy can be difficult for Eights because intimacy is based on allowing yourself to be vulnerable.

Nines are at the middle point of the gut center. They don't want anyone to control them, but they don't like conflicts which may occur from openly expressing their opinion if they try to assert themselves. Even though they are at the middle point of the gut center, they are very easy to get along with and show very little anger with the exception of occasional eruptions. Most of the time Nines *dull* or narcotize their anger to avoid the anxiety caused by conflict.

Ones do what they think they are *supposed* to do. They direct their anger toward others indirectly as criticism, and only infrequently release it in explosive outbursts. Generally their anger is *imploded*, directed inward, and it drives them to think critically and obsessively about and pursue some special idealistic belief.

THE CONTROLLER
TYPE EIGHT

"Tell it like it is!... Get mad *and* get back!...Stand up for yourself!...Sure something went wrong, and it's *your* fault!...I'll protect you...Go for it!...Don't try to control me!...I like a person who can stand up and fight for their rights...It's my way or the highway..." These statements, reflecting issues of power, confrontation, blaming and control, are the flavor of the Type Eight personality. They are the bosses, leaders, dominators and protectors.

Gurdjieff, who brought the Enneagram to the West, was a Type Eight. His approach to personal growth was very aggressive, and he was very demanding and hard on his students. Frank Sinatra, who does what he wants, gets what he wants, and sings songs like "My Way," appears to be a Type Eight. Mike Tyson, the boxer, is a member of the Eight community.

The **compelling desire** of Type Eights is to feel powerful and have control over their lives. Being in control helps them to avoid being taken advantage of, to avoid appearing weak and to avoid feeling their vulnerable and sensitive inner world.

ASSOCIATED DESIRES

Their **associated desires** include a desire to exhibit power, get whatever they want, control their space, to confront, and to seek justice.

EXHIBIT POWER

All Type Eights exhibit power to avoid appearing weak and feeling vulnerable. Some Eights exhibit their power internally in the form of self-control, and some Eights exhibit power externally in the form of controlling others. Some are introverts and some are extroverts. The introverted Eights use their power to carefully control their behavior and often appear passive and at ease, whereas the extroverted Eights overtly exhibit their power, often flamboyantly, to feel in control of the situation.

Extroverted Eights, in their need to exhibit power, appear arrogant and domineering. They want people to respect them and see their power. These Eights don't like to be ignored. They regard tactful and cautious approaches to situations as a sign of weakness. Displaying power helps to keep themselves and others from seeing their inner vulnerability.

The open expression of anger is often essential to their exhibition of power. Many Eights are proud that their anger is easily aroused and directly expressed. However, they don't like the feedback which they often get that they are "always" angry. These Eights feel misunderstood. Other Eights have become aware that unrestrained and open displays of anger cause them to be less in control so they try to exert self-control over their anger.

Eights are proud of their capacity to face physical pain. Many Eights were physically abused as children and have developed an unusual capacity to block painful sensations in their body.

Like many Type Fours, many Eights like to live on the edge and to push their limits. Boredom and self-doubt can set in when they aren't pushing and testing. They often push the limits of the law or break the law. They tend to be contemptuous of society's laws and rules. Some may drive a fast motorcycle or participate in other high-risk activities to feel and exhibit their fearlessness.

Extroverted Eights will frequently push and test my limits during a class session to see how I will react. "Is he weak or strong? What is his response to my show of power? Can I trust him? What can I get away with?"

Most people establish an intimate and trusting understanding of others by sharing vulnerabilities. In the beginning of a relationship, Eights build a closer trusting relationship than other types by developing a comfort level. The comfort level comes from the expression of their power and the testing of the other person's response to their exhibition of power. Eights are the people who frequently become good friends with someone they have just fought with intensely.

Exhibiting power also protects them from feeling vulnerable. As one Eight said, "I hate feeling vulnerable. To me, that's when people will take advantage of me the most." It is difficult for Eights to trust others. Trust is "giving up control." Their sensitivity about trust causes them to become very upset if someone lies to them.

This fear of vulnerability and their lack of trust makes relationships difficult. "Relationships are difficult for me because of my lack of trust in people. Sure I test them, but most people never pass the test well enough for me to relax. Who knows, maybe when I meet that special person I'll be able to knock down my wall," reported a Type Eight. When they feel safe in a relationship and are in a private space, the "ferocious bull dog" can become a cuddly puppy.

This show of power is subtly energetic as well as often openly exhibitionistic and confrontive. When a group of Eights share their personality type in front of a class or workshop, class members can *feel* their power. The class will often fidget and display other signs of discomfort when they experience the intimidating energy of a group of Eights.

GET WHATEVER THEY WANT

Eights don't take no for an answer. They are lustful and go forcefully after whatever they want, whether it's sex, money or power. They don't always get what they want, but it isn't because they don't try, and they don't give up easily. They feel they can get whatever it is they want and they like challenges. This tenacity is a factor in why many Eights become leaders.

Very unhealthy Eights can be cunning and deceptive in their quest to fulfill their desires. They will lie, cheat and steal with absolutely no feelings of guilt. People are simply objects to be manipulated and used. Even for many normal Eights, guilt is foreign. After hearing this statement, one Eight seemed surprised and asked, "Do any Eights ever feel guilty?" Another

Type Eight resented the statement about lack of guilt and said, "I do have a conscience about what is right and wrong. And I try to do the right thing. But I certainly don't feel guilty if I do the wrong thing."

CONFRONT

They are confrontive and aren't interested in understanding other people's points of view when it conflicts with theirs. They like to speak openly and directly, and appreciate others who don't "beat around the bush." This confrontive approach, if it doesn't scare you, can be a refreshing encounter with someone who is communicating in an uncomplicated and direct manner. Most people are uncomfortable with the Eights' directness and are annoyed by their need to be seen and to show and test their power.

Eights don't just enjoy verbal confrontations, they often thrive on them. Confrontations aren't just to win or to make a point, but they also help Eights to feel their own power. As one Eight reported, "It's fun for me to go against someone I feel is a worthy opponent."

What makes confrontation with Eights upsetting to many people is their tendency to lay trips on others, blame the other person and to rationalize their own inappropriate behavior. The consistent and forceful tone of a verbal confrontation with a Type Eight includes statements like "I am totally" right, and you are "totally" wrong.

CONTROL THEIR OWN SPACE

Their confrontations and exhibitions of power are part of their effort to control their own space. They try to dominate their environment and rebel against anyone who tries to control them. They rebel against people, cultures and even slightly controlling situations. For example, in classes and workshops, Type Six, the Loyal-skeptic and Type Eight, the Controller, are the two types who have great difficulty identifying their personality type.

The Loyal-skeptic experiences difficulties for the obvious

reason of doubtfulness. However, the Controller's reasons are more subtle. Most Eights are proud to be typed as an Eight. However, some feel that people will reject them if it's known that they are an Eight.

Being typed is also viewed as a form of being controlled for many Eights, even if they are the one doing the self-analysis and typing. When I first started teaching the Enneagram, I suggested to a Type Eight who asked me what his personality type was that I thought he could possibly be a Type Eight personality. His response was, "I know that I'm not an Eight. I'm probably a One or a Three. If someone could identify your personality type, they could control you." After several weeks he became more trusting about the environment and was able to accurately describe himself as a Type Eight.

Eights feel that even an apparently small loss of control can easily escalate into a greater loss of control, so they strive to control every detail of their life and the lives of influential people in their environment.

This need to control their own space is also due to their difficulty in trusting the intentions of other people. Other people are often viewed as threats to their power and control. They are always very aware of who the powerful people are in their environment.

Sex is another way which they exhibit power, control their space and get what they want. It is a way to reassure the Eight of their power, be intimate for a limited amount of time and yet not be controlled. Sex involves a fixed duration of intimate contact, so control is only momentarily lost, if at all. Sex for an Eight often represents the submission of the other person to the Eight's power.

SEEK JUSTICE

The justice that Eights believe in is their own definition of justice. At an unconscious level Eights often feel they were unfairly and unjustly treated as children and therefore feel justified in doing whatever they can get away with. They don't live by the rules. They make the rules.

If someone "crosses" them, they feel justified in being punitive and vengeful. Eights will often spend months or even years getting back to make the person who betrayed them feel the pain which they experienced when they were betrayed and to reassure themselves of their power and capacity to control. As an extreme example of Type Eight vengeance, one very successful Type Eight businesswoman said that she plotted for several years to kill a former business partner who had cheated her. She only gave up the idea of killing him when she found out she could put him in prison for fraud.

Healthier Eights often take pride in protecting others who are weak or treated unjustly. "I have a great deal of empathy for people unable to stand up for themselves, particularly young people who have been victimized," reported one Type Eight. Healthy Eights are often powerful leaders in the promotion of rights for minorities or the underprivileged. A cause gives them purpose and justifies their expression of power and control.

In relationships, Eights will often provide a protective shield from the outside world for their friends. One Type Eight reported, "My friends know that I will be there for them and protect them."

WINGS OF A EIGHT

When an Eight leans toward the Nine Type, the edge is taken off their aggressive tendencies.

When an Eight leans in the direction of a Type Seven, the Eight's powerful and lustful nature is combined with the Seven's optimistic nature and leads to an optimistic and forceful search for fun.

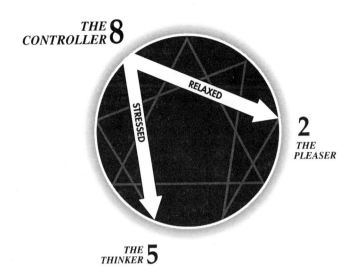

THE **8**
CONTROLLER

RELAXED

STRESSED

2
THE
PLEASER

THE **5**
THINKER

STRESS AND RELAXATION

When **STRESSED** Eights can't assert control in their normally direct way, they become incredible rationalizers as they move to Point Five on the Enneagram. They can rationalize and justify any behavior and are clever at making their justification believable. They can also be cold and calculating when stressed, planning some clever way to get back at someone whom they feel has hurt them.

Eights feel relaxed when they feel safe and in control. Their shift to the Two Point on the Enneagram when **RELAXED** exposes a very vulnerable, giving and protective dimension of their personality. To get to this safe, relaxed state in a personal relationship, the Eight puts the other person through many tests to make sure they won't be taken advantage of once they relax. One Type Eight reported, "I'm an incredibly giving person once I trust the person I'm interacting with."

Even in this "relaxed" state, Eights are very alert to criticism and rejection and are very possessive of the person they've tested and found to be trustworthy. Another Eight said, "I have a lot of love and affection to give, but don't underestimate me. I don't let anyone run my life." So, even when an Eight moves to the Two Point, they don't completely let down their defenses.

RECOGNIZING A TYPE EIGHT

Type Eights usually stand erect and have firm, solid bodies, even when they are overweight. They tend to be arrogant, intimidating and confrontive. If something does not work out right, they get angry and blame you.

Their eyes often appear cool, or they display a disarming light-heartedness. They are appraising you and the situation. When you are around them, you tend to feel that you should be careful and cautious.

It is virtually impossible to convince them to change their position in an argument, especially if it involves who is at fault. If you tune into your bodily senses, you can feel their power filling the space around them and you.

SUB-TYPES OF A TYPE EIGHT

INTIMATE RELATIONSHIPS:
POSSESSION AND SURRENDER

It isn't easy for most people to remember that inside the tough exterior of a Type Eight is a vulnerable child who doesn't want to be taken advantage of. However, this inner vulnerability is exactly why an Eight will repeatedly test someone with whom they want an intimate relationship. Once they are satisfied that the person is trustworthy and won't take unfair advantage of them, they can safely surrender their need to be constantly in control. But then, they want to possess this safe and trustworthy person and to keep them forever.

Leaving an intimate relationship with a Type Eight is usually very difficult and in some cases can be life-threatening. "Before I can give myself to a relationship, I have to feel that it is safe to do so. This requires my mate to pass test after test after test. Once he's passed the tests, then I become possessive, because I know how hard it was to find him," explained one Type Eight.

SOCIAL RELATIONSHIPS:
FRIENDSHIP

Friendship for a Social Relationship Eight is based on mutual protection. They are loyal friends with those whom they protect and those who protect them.

SELF-PRESERVATION:
BEING IN CONTROL

Avoiding vulnerability by being in control of their immediate surroundings is the preoccupation of a Self-Preservation Eight. Their hypersensitivity to anyone's effort to control them is their most important first line of defense for survival and avoiding feeling vulnerable.

THE PEACEMAKER TYPE NINE

"It doesn't matter...No big deal...Don't get upset, we can resolve this calmly...Nothing bothers me...What's all the fuss about?...Whatever you want to do is fine with me...I can fit in anywhere," are statements by Nines which reveal their need to be at ease and to avoid conflict. These are the dependable, difficult-to-upset co-workers and spouses, the steady and unshakable friends and the easygoing, yet oftentimes dull and stubborn people who want peace at any price. They are often accountants or engineers.

General Norman Schwarzkopf, the general who was the military leader during the Gulf War, is exemplary of the Type Nine personality. Being steady and easygoing, he was able to lead methodically the many diverse nations and different military personalities involved in winning the Persian Gulf war. Carl Rogers, the easygoing, humanistic psychologist, was a Type Nine. His last major effort before he died was to promote world peace and teach methods of conflict resolution. President Bill Clinton is also a Type Nine.

The **compelling desire** for a Nine is to be at peace with themselves and the world. They desire a quiet, effortless, and easygoing life. They want to avoid anger because it could disrupt the peace and lead to internal and external conflict. They seem to have no will of their own and they submit to the will of others because they want to avoid conflict.

ASSOCIATED DESIRES

Associated with this compelling desire for peace are the *associated desires* to avoid anger, avoid conflict, maintain the status quo, change slowly and merge with others.

AVOID ANGER

Nines have avoided anger so long and so effectively that they are very resistant to the idea that they repress their anger. "Who, me? I'm rarely angry!" Unconsciously they are always angry.

Anger is a strong feeling of displeasure. Displeasure and the easygoing lifestyle of a Nine don't go hand in hand. Anger suggests that you disagree and have your own independent opinion. Children in the "terrible two's" stage say no to almost everything as they begin asserting their independence. Nines, because they are not comfortable asserting their own opinions and saying no, give into the needs of others. It is easier to submit to others than to be aware of and satisfy their own needs.

Nines deaden angry feelings by sleeping, watching television, overeating and/or using drugs. They avoid conflict by being stubborn or compliant. When they do things, it's generally out of obligation to someone else rather than out of commitment to some personal goal. The repressed anger is sometimes triggered by a minor incident and produces a major outburst. The image of a volcano exploding is representative of their infrequent yet powerful eruptions of anger.

Splitting off their awareness is another way to avoid anger. When you talk to a Nine, you often get the feeling that they are not present. And they frequently aren't present. "I am a bad listener at times. I tend to start daydreaming or thinking of things that I need to do when people are talking to me," reported one Type Nine.

Except for an occasional explosion of anger to vent their inner resentment and hostility, Nines rarely show anger. However, they exhibit anger indirectly by being stubborn. They are, in effect, saying "I can't say no to your needs, but I can at least make you work hard to get me to say yes." Type Nine is one of the most stubborn types on the Enneagram.

Nines drain a lot of their energy to contain their anger, leaving little energy and enthusiasm to pursue life. To avoid conflict, most of the energy available after containing their own anger is used to help others meet their needs. When Nines do release their anger, it is often in a socially acceptable way such as contact sports where they feel extra-alive, vital and for a short time in touch with themselves.

AVOID CONFLICT

Another reason that Nines have trouble saying no is that it runs the risk of open anger, abandonment, and shattering of their peaceful life. At a more subtle level, Nines often enter a psychological union with another person and experience the other person's needs as their own. Saying no to a person they are in union with is like saying no to themselves. Blocking someone else's needs is experienced as blocking *their own* needs.

There is a saying, "If you can't say no then you can't say yes." So Nines, because they have difficulty saying no, are more often compliant rather than enthusiastic. As a result, Nines are often viewed as dull and lackluster. They avoid arguments, saying, "Let's talk about this logically and calmly." They will run away from arguments or try to get them over quickly. "I want to get this settled and over with fast!"

When verbally attacked, Nines will tend to diffuse the intensity of the attack and their response by a quick, unconscious broadening and rationalizing of what the verbal attack is about. If someone says "I HATE YOU!" to a Nine, the Nine immediately and automatically is understanding. They unconsciously rationalize the other person's behavior by thinking things such as: "They don't really hate me, they are out of control and confused; I need to be understanding." This allows the Nine to avoid becoming visibly or consciously angry. Nines tend to minimize problems hoping that the problems will just pass or fade away.

Feelings and problems can arouse anger and conflict, so Nines keep them to themselves. "I'm not very open, and I keep most of my feelings to myself, and that bothers people around me. People who care about me ask me to say what is on my mind. But I don't really believe that they want to know how I feel." Nine's don't share their feelings freely, and when they do share feelings, they are usually only positive ones, unless their angry volcano is erupting. "If I have problems, I feel like they are my problems, and I don't want to share them with others. I do try to share my loving feelings."

Nines like to be viewed as good and nice, but this is really a way to avoid anger and conflict. Doing nothing is one way Nines are nice. Many Nines show their love for their spouse by doing nothing. They deaden awareness of their own needs and don't tune into the needs of their spouse. They become deadened, bored, and boring, but nice.

MAINTAIN THE STATUS QUO

Nines are very habitual and steady. They thrive on routine. They behave as if they were in a trance or asleep. But by narcotizing their anger, they deaden their passion for life. They are uninterested in and unaware of their own needs. They are easily satisfied with, and resigned to, small rewards in life.

The gut is the center for strength as well as anger. Even though Nines can be very strong for others, they tend to be weak and indecisive when it comes to meeting their own needs. Their needs were overlooked by their parents, and they overlook their own needs as adults. They stood no chance of having their needs met and were discounted in childhood, so why should they expect anything for themselves now? They settle for crumbs from the banquet of life. As a Nine expressed it, "It doesn't take much to make me happy."

Even when they do feel a spark of desire, it is easily and quickly deadened or diverted. They are easily distracted from their own priorities to assuming someone else's, or they get involved in some mundane detail or another less important project. The speed of their diversion can be heard in their speech. When they express an important thought, the most important part of the message is delivered within the first few words, sentence or paragraph. Then their voice trails off. Their energy fades and they lose interest in what they are saying and stop or change the subject.

CHANGE SLOWLY

If they do move from the status quo, it is very slow, deliberate and you guessed it: conflict-free. The time required for them to change jobs or a committed relationship can be measured in years or decades. I knew one Nine who planned his divorce for six years after he had decided to leave his wife. He told me how proud he was when his attorney told him that his divorce was the smoothest divorce that he had ever encountered. Every detail had been planned with utmost concern for timing and fairness to his wife and four children.

MERGE WITH OTHERS

Another way Nines avoid anger and conflict and lose contact with their own needs is to merge with others. The distinction between their needs and those of the other person become indistinguishable. They sacrifice their own needs for the needs of others. During childhood they felt frustrated and hopeless in asserting their own needs, and eventually they gave up even being aware of their own needs and settled for living through satisfying the needs of others. They comply with others' expectations and try to make the other person's dreams come true. If and when Nines wake up to their own needs, they realize that they have, in effect, been living out someone else's life.

Because Nines can easily understand other people's needs and point of view, it is usually at the expense of their own loss of self-understanding, and they are often ambivalent and indecisive. If they care about the feelings of more than one person at a time, they feel frustrated and pulled in too many directions. To avoid feeling angry, they postpone making a decision and/or deaden themselves to avoid the need to decide. While procrastinating, their indecisiveness and fear of too many options lead them to obsessive thinking about what the right decision should be.

They are very accepting and trusting of other people and generous in helping them to lead enjoyable, conflict-free lives. They are more capable of providing others with what they want than they are in providing for themselves. They often over-trust people. One Type Nine stated, "I've been told that I trust people too much or think everyone is a good person."

Nines can be very accommodating when meeting the needs of others. As children they were unknowingly forced to give in to the needs of their parents, and their need to avoid conflict and anger combined with the feeling of powerlessness (impotence) left them unable to strive forcefully to actualize their own needs. They over-adjust to the needs of other people. "Sometimes I tend to go along with what other people want me to do and end up doing things I don't really care to do. I also don't always tell people when something is bothering me until it gets so out of hand that I break down and unload everything."

As teachers, they give into the needs of their students. As bosses, they give into the needs of their employees. As therapists, they are overly concerned about their clients needs. As spouses, they are more concerned about their spouse's needs than their own needs.

WINGS OF A NINE

Nines' wings are Types One and Eight. The Nines that lean toward the One Wing are judgmental, obsessive thinkers, and always trying to improve. Nines leaning toward the Eight Wing are more aggressive and controlling.

If a Nine does not lean toward either the Eight or the One Wing, they are torn between these two Wings. On the one hand they want to be like a One and do what they are supposed to do, to do what is right. On the other hand, they want to be like an Eight and do whatever they want to do. You can see why Nines can be immobilized and on the fence about important issues because of this internal conflict.

STRESS AND RELAXATION

When Nines are **STRESSED**, whether from conflict, illness, or too much work, they move to Type Six on the Enneagram. Their inner feelings of helplessness and impotence emerge. They become doubtful about their capacity to achieve or relate in life.

When a Nine is feeling **RELAXED** or loving, some of their constricted energy is released, and they move to Type Three on the Enneagram. They become a Nine flavored with a desire to achieve and become productive.

They don't work out of a fear of failure like a Type Three. A Nine in love and relaxed will work hard for their loved ones or society as a way to express their love. And, like Type Threes, they may suffer from physical burnout if they remain at the Three Point too long.

RECOGNIZING A NINE

Nines' energy is normally subdued. They dress conservatively and habitually. They are very accommodating to the desires of others. They tend to be viewed as peaceful, easygoing, accepting and responsible people. They are patient and helpful.

When you ask them a question, they tend to respond by telling a "heroic" story and go off on some tangent. When they are listening to you, if you watch their eyes carefully you will notice that they tend to split their attention between you and some other thought or fantasy. Their speech is usually slow and lacks vitality because they tend to be thinking about what they are saying while they are talking rather than trying to influence you in some way.

SUB-TYPES OF THE NINE TYPE

INTIMATE RELATIONSHIPS: UNION

Intimate Nines unite, melt, or merge with significant others. They have difficulty separating their desires, fears, and interests from that of the other person. In effect, they get lost in the other person. When this happens, it is very difficult for them to leave a relationship, because in a way it is like leaving themselves. They prefer one-on-one relationships. They often seek partners who won't control them or who are more in touch with their feelings and more energetic.

SOCIAL RELATIONSHIPS:
JOINERS

Social Nines tend to join clubs, churches or other groups of interest to them. Although they join organizations, they tend to hang out on the fringe, not fully involved yet still a member of the group. The energy of the group enlivens them, and yet they can remain on the edge so they aren't controlled or absorbed by the group.

SELF-PRESERVATION:
CONSUMPTION

A self-preservation Nine tries to dull unconscious anger and conflict by consuming large amounts of drink and food, or becoming overly involved in hobbies and activities which distract them from their inner feelings and real needs.

If food is their narcotizing agent, they are often overweight. Food never satisfies their hunger because they aren't hungry for food. They are hungry to avoid conflict and anger.

THE PERFECTIONIST TYPE ONE

"Tell me exactly what you want...Don't say that I am perfect. I'm not, I could improve a lot...There is a better way...If you would only try harder...I could have...I should...I ought to work harder...Seek excellence in everything you do..." These are the people who believe that they can always do more and strive to be better. They are relentlessly trying to improve themselves and others. Their expectations in important aspects of their life are very high. As one Type One said, "My expectations are always just out of reach."

The **compelling desire** of a Type One is to avoid mistakes, do what is right and pursue their high ideals. They seek perfection in areas of their life where they feel they have the ideal, perfect and correct vision of what should be. The driving force behind their desires is their inner critic, energized by inner-directed anger and fear of being judged by other people. "If I am perfect, no one will criticize me, and I won't need to be so tough on myself. I can relax." In reality, they can never relax because their expectations are so high that they can never be achieved. These are the precise and careful English teachers, dentists, accountants and preachers.

The strength of the desire to be perfect reflects the intensity of the fear which they have of their own angry judgmental mind, more than a positive desire to achieve perfection. The greater the fear, the greater the drive for perfection, and the higher the expectations and the less chance of feeling good. Like the desires of every personality type, the desires for perfection are never achieved.

Margaret Thatcher, Martin Luther King and Ralph Nader exemplify the high ideals of the Type One. They also exemplify the relentless, careful, efficient, hard working, reformer attitude of the Type One.

ASSOCIATED DESIRES

The **associated desires** for a One are to perfect important aspects of their life, reform other people, avoid expressing anger and avoid making mistakes. All of their associated drives are energized by the same driving force: avoidance of the inner critic and criticism from others.

PERFECT AN ASPECT OF LIFE

Ones have an all-or-nothing attitude about things they do. So, they don't strive for perfection in everything they do. Most Ones seek perfection in selected areas of life and neglect other areas. A Type One personality who is a teacher wrote, "In the classroom I am well-organized and efficient, but you should see my home!"

Usually their high expectations are related to their career, family or some moral or ethical issue. A good example of a Type One personality is the television preacher who has every hair in place, a mechanically perfect presentation and "my way is the only way and the right way" attitude.

Being in control and striving for perfection helps Ones to relax and avoid criticism. A Type One related, "This inclination to seek perfection gives me a sense of control in my life. I can determine what I make of myself if I strive hard enough. When I lack a sense of being in control, I am tense, anxious and worry too much. The more control I feel, the more relaxed I become."

Ones strive for perfection but never feel perfect. As one woman remarked, "The other night my boss told me that he saw an episode of the 'Oprah Winfrey Show' about women who always look very put together. I was shocked when he told me that he thought of me while watching the program. I must admit that I am never satisfied with myself, whether it be my appearance, my grades, or my whole self-concept. This is probably the part of my personality where my 'One-ness' shows the most. I tend to not only be judgmental, but extremely hard on myself to the point of depression."

Like Threes, Ones work hard, but unlike Threes they need to do things properly, not just get things done. As one Type One wrote, "Once my mind is set to do something, it will get done. I always feel uncomfortable leaving a job unfinished. You can rely on me to be punctual. I see how it is when other people are always late and it doesn't appeal to me. I know other people like to work with me because the job gets done, and done right, so both of us feel good about ourselves." At some level, she is aware that her work and doing it right have more to do with self-worth than achievement.

Some Ones get carried away with perfection. One Type One I knew carefully vacuumed not only the house and garage on a daily basis, but also the rafters in the garage.

REFORM OTHERS

Ones like to reform others and encourage them to develop the same standards and beliefs they have. They feel morally superior. Their conscious goal is to help others live a better life. However, it's their superior and unattainable vision of life which they want others to achieve. Ones help to "save" other people from the inner turmoil and guilt which they feel they themselves would suffer if they exchanged places. In other words, Ones project their own fear of judgment onto other people. They reform to make the world more perfect according to their own image of perfection.

The same demands which they place on themselves are placed on others. "I feel like a failure whenever I don't excel at something, which, of course, is very self-destructive and also keeps me from trying new things. If I visit some other individuals home which is not immaculate, or if they serve dinner late, I feel like they have failed as a homemaker. In short, I'm much too hard on myself and I expect too much of other people, too".

AVOID EXPRESSING ANGER

Anger is repressed by Ones and vented indirectly in the form of criticism or an arrogant, superior attitude. They try to be extra nice to avoid revealing hostile feelings. However, the anger in their demand for perfection and their judgmental attitude toward those who do not reform shines through in their rigid facial expression and body posture.

Critical remarks provide an outlet for anger. One perfectionist remarked, "As a perfectionist, it is easy for me to be critical and make 'smart aleck' remarks because I know that I am **absolutely** right!"

They are unconsciously resentful for having had to comply to such high standards since childhood. They work so hard to achieve the unachievable standards that they have little time or energy left to become aware of or to satisfy their own real needs. The resulting resentment is a symptom of repressed anger. But the open expression of anger is considered bad, so they must be absolutely correct and right in order to vent it. "I think very carefully before an argument to make sure I'm right and to keep people from getting the best of me."

Having high standards and "black and white" beliefs are major motivations for Type Ones. It doesn't mar their perfect self-concept when they are critical, judgmental, argumentive and impatient with people who don't live up to their standards or agree with them. And because their beliefs are unreasonably narrow and standards unreasonably high, they can vent this "justifiable" and disguised anger at almost anyone. Arguing with a One is a no-win situation. Their position has been carefully thought through, and they "know" there is only one correct answer, and it is theirs. And, after all, one of the main underlying reasons for the argument is to provide a justifiable venting of their anger and resentment.

AVOID MAKING MISTAKES

As children they were painfully criticized, and as adults everything, every decision, every comment, every action is a "big deal" to a One. They don't want to be judged internally or externally by others for making mistakes. Their inner critic is considered to be correct, better and wiser than the rest of their personality.

This "valued" inner critic can make Ones worry about everything. Many Ones worry about avoiding mistakes in the future and wonder if they did the right thing in the past. "I feel that it is necessary to save for the future so that I will be financially secure. I worry needlessly that I will lose my job and its added security, or that my boyfriend will leave me and I will be without a secure relationship. My worries gives me a lot of stress, and everyone tells me that they are without reason and just a waste of time. The stresses in my life are made by me, however, they are very much a reality."

"If I worry enough, I can prevent errors in the future" is part of the rationale behind preventive worrying. Difficulty sleeping and difficulty relaxing are two of the by-products of excessive worrying and carefulness.

Ones see their own faults easily. To avoid judgment by others and internal judgement, Ones attempt to be blameless. Part of their approach to feeling blameless is to see other's faults just as bad, if not worse, than their own. Focusing their critical energy on others and trying to reform them helps Ones focus their judgment externally.

Most Ones live publicly straight and sexually constrained lives. The inner critic judges them harshly for any sexual feelings, so they tend to vent their sexual energy using brief "back door" relationships of intense sexuality. A country like Sweden is very conservative and perfectionistic, and yet Swedes maintain a liberal outlook toward sex. Many Ones in Sweden live a "double life" and provide their own sexual outlet by using a "back door" to have affairs or visit prostitutes. During these brief encounters they can temporarily fend off the inner critic.

Ones think to themselves, "If I am perfect, I won't make any mistakes, and I hate to do something twice," and "I will do the right thing, then I will be accepted, loved and can relax." This desire to be perfect is driven by guilt, anxiety, and fear of self-rejection. They constantly strive to improve, be right, and do the right things.

WORK HARD PLAY LATER

Ones aren't usually aware that they postpone pleasure. Their priority in life is to work toward perfection. "You can have fun after you've done what you are supposed to do," is a common childhood message for a One. " 'Before you can go out and play this weekend, I want your room spotless, including your closet.' Every Saturday morning I would hear the familiar phrase from my mother," reported another Type One. "It became routine for me to spend half an hour to forty-five minutes straightening, dusting, and vacuuming my bedroom before my mother's careful inspection. Upon approval, I could be free to do as I pleased. This 'clean first, play second' rule enforced over and over again by an angry mother helped me down the primrose path of a One personality."

In reality, play, fun and pleasure rarely arrive. The compelling drive of the perfectionist, like all compelling drives, are never achievable and never ending. Many Ones die before play, fun or pleasure ever occurs. However, in a sense it is O.K. for Ones because they feel they are doing the "right thing".

WINGS OF A ONE

Ones leaning in the direction of their Two wing will be softer and more supportive. Their reforming will have a more nurturing tone. The Ones colored by their Nine wing are not as energetic about reform and less critical of others.

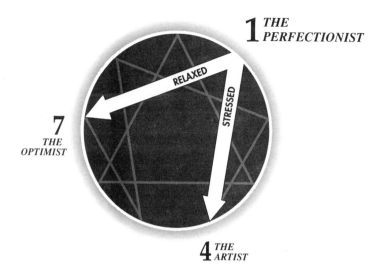

STRESS AND RELAXATION

When **STRESSED** Ones move to the Four Point and become melancholic about what could have or should have occurred in their lives. They experience depressing and tragic feelings about their futile efforts to achieve high ideals and do the right thing.

When **RELAXED** Ones move to Point Seven and become light-hearted and preoccupied with optimistic plans for future fun. However, these plans usually remain just plans because their needs to be perfect dominate their life. If they do take a vacation or attempt to do something fun, they make sure they do what they are supposed to do on the vacation. Unlike Type Sevens, they are less flexible and must stick to their vacation plans even if they aren't enjoying them. At least they can avoid the inner critic if they stick to their plans.

RECOGNIZING A TYPE ONE

This rigidity of thinking is visible in their over-control of their body and speech. A tight upper lip or pursed mouth reveals their effort to control their expression and their life. Lecturing with the intent to reform you is what stands out in their communication. People tend to feel inferior and judged when around a Type One. They are organized and efficient in their communication as well as the rest of their life. They often groom to perfection.

SUB-TYPES OF A TYPE ONE

INTIMATE RELATIONSHIPS:
JEALOUSY

Their partner's behavior is observed carefully. Anything which does or could threaten the relationship is critically judged. Other people can be targets of intensely jealous judging. This jealousy is an outlet for the repressed anger directed at someone who is threatening their "perfect relationship."

SOCIAL RELATIONSHIPS:
INADAPTABILITY

Inadaptability arises due to their rigid social position, usually concerning a moral issue. They believe they are right and will stand firm and defend their position. If they are to attend a party that doesn't start on time, or go according to plan, a Social Relations Type One will display their inflexibility by complaining and perhaps leaving.

SELF-PRESERVATION: WORRY

Self-preservation Ones are anxious and worry about being "good enough" and how to avoid making mistakes that would cripple their ability to survive. Their belief is that if they constantly (obsessively) think (worry) about the immediate and distant future, they can prevent negative consequences. For example, a sixteen-year-old Type One personality I know worries about finances for retirement. "I worry too much. I worry that I may not be good enough in what I do, because what I do must be perfect. I worry that I might not earn enough money to support my family and myself. And even if there was enough money, I would still worry. I would worry that I might make a mistake that would jeopardize our survival."

Now that we've explored the nine personality types, we will look at child development to discover how your personality was developed.

CHAPTER
9

MORE ABOUT CHILDHOOD

A brief introduction to how you developed your personality in early childhood was presented in Chapter One. Chapter Nine will provide greater depth and clarity about the development of your personality type. It lays the foundation for understanding your most important relationships, because the way you related to your environment and especially your parent(s) as a child has an enormous effect on who you relate to and how you relate to them now as an adult.

In the womb and during the first few years of your childhood your personality type was virtually completely formed and rigidified. Your personality determines how you function in the world.

You developed your personality type in order to relate to your parent(s) and exist in the world. The health of the personality type which you developed depended primarily on the psychological health of the people doing the parenting when you were an infant. Your personality is something which you refined to live within a specific, limited, prenatal and early childhood environment. The good news is that if it's something which you help to create, you can also modify and improve it in order to find love and fulfillment in your life and the world within which you now live.

What would happen if you destroyed or lost your personality? What, if anything, is beneath its protective shell? How could you relate to others without your personality? Some of this chapter and a large portion of Part Three of this book refers to your essence. Your essence, that which is most true and real in you, lies within the shell of the personality. When the shell is softened and relaxed, your essence can begin to emerge and express itself through your personality. You become more whole and your life becomes more rewarding.

A brief introduction to the extremely complex and controversial topic of personality development is provided in this chapter. Parent and child capacities, recovery from childhood, loss of essence, birth order, genetics, theories of traditional Enneagram teachers, personality differences, object relations theory and specific Enneagram personality type development are discussed.

Whether you were raised primarily by both parents or one parent, a relative or older sibling, when the word parent is used in this book it refers to your primary caretaker and your childhood environment in general.

The discussion of theories of childhood which follows isn't intended to place blame or praise on parents or anyone else for their behavior or for yours. We are all living the healthiest life we can, based on our inborn traits and our past and present environments. The intent of this discussion is to help you grow by gaining a clearer understanding of how your personality developed, so you can grow and expand more quickly and easily.

PARENT AND CHILD CAPACITIES

Our all-too-human parents with all-too-human limitations raised their children in the best way they knew how, just as their parents raised them the best way they knew how. A psychologically limited parent cannot raise very healthy children. The capacity to see their children accurately and to support and raise them according to their unique needs is limited for all parents because all parents raise their children utilizing their particular personalities. To make your understanding of how your personality was development even more difficult to understand, both mom and dad usually have different and often opposite personality types. Therefore, conflict on how to raise their children is inevitable. Also, when you were a child your environment could have been unsupportive, your parents may have been suffering from ill health, experiencing financial difficulties or living in a country which was at war.

All of these environmental factors influenced the quality of your upbringing. In spite of all these variables, psychologically healthier parents generally raise psychologically healthier children. Thankfully, most parents have grown psychologically more healthy, live in a better environment and are more secure financially than their parents. As a result, they tend to parent better than they were parented and their children are somewhat more psychologically healthy.

As children, we learn to block most of our essence and behave in ways which get us the most love and approval and the least physical and emotional pain. For example, some parents only give love in the form of praise to their children when they achieve. These children, who want love and acceptance, learn very early that the only way to get love is to achieve, or at least to try to look like an Achiever. They focus their energy, their attention and their life toward achievement. The billionaire industrialist, Malcolm Forbes, when asked how he achieved so much in life, replied "I was lucky. I was born into the right family."

Achievers are often wealthy. However, they always pay a personal penalty. They become separated from and forget their essential capacities such as the capacity for love, truth, curiosity, compassion and expansiveness. As adults, they mistakenly believed that this protective, survival-oriented fixated personality shell, which developed early in childhood, is all that there is to themselves. They identify with their limited, constricted personality and can't completely enjoy their life or their wealth. They have a lifestyle instead of a life.

Our parenting style depends to a great extent on the mental

health of our parents and on how we were raised. We will usually observe and **copy** their style of parenting or use a completely **opposite** style. Even if we don't like the way we were raised, we are likely to raise our children the same way. Research shows that people who are physically abused as children are more likely than average to abuse their children or else go to the other extreme and not discipline them at all. At a lighter level, people who received few gifts from their parents as children either give their children few gifts or overindulge them with gifts.

EXPERIENCING CHILDHOOD

No matter how well you were parented your personality will not be as developed as it could be and most of your awareness of your essence will be blocked. No parents are perfect and all infants are fragile. And, as we will discuss more in Part Three, if you are conditioned to develop an unhealthy personality as a child, it doesn't mean that you are stuck with it forever.

Abraham Maslow, the founder of Humanistic Psychology, was born in a Brooklyn, New York, slum district. He was raised by unhealthy parents, a schizophrenic mother and a father who was disgusted with his wife, his mother gave birth to seven children. His father spent his time drinking, fighting and chasing women. Maslow was afraid of him. Maslow said, "I was awfully curious to find out why I didn't go insane. I was certainly neurotic, extremely neurotic, during all my first twenty years - depressed, terribly unhappy, lonely, isolated, self-rejecting, and so on - but in theory it should have been much worse. And so I traced it back and found that my mother's brother - my maternal uncle, who's a very kind and good man to this day, and who lived nearby – took care of me. He liked babies and children and simply took care of us whenever my mother got herself a new baby. He may have saved my life, physically." (audio tape made by Maslow and reported in Colin Wilson's book *New Pathways in Psychology; Maslow and the Post-Freudian Revolution.*)

If your parents did their best to parent and you did your best as a child to get your needs met, how is it that you become so removed from your essence, your true nature? In a letter to psychologist Karen Horney, one of her patients describes the process very well.

"How is it possible to lose a self (essence)? The treachery, unknown and unthinkable, begins with our secret, psychic death in childhood - if and when we are not loved and are cut off from our spontaneous wishes...It is a perfect double crime in which... the tiny self gradually and unwittingly takes part. He has not been accepted for him, as he is. Oh, they love him, but they want him or force him or expect him to be different! Therefore *he must be unacceptable.* He himself learns to believe it and at last even takes it for granted. He has truly given himself up. No matter now whether he obeys them, whether he clings, rebels or withdraws – his behavior and his performance is all that matters. His center of gravity is in them, not in himself - yet if he so much as noticed it he would think it natural enough. And the whole thing is entirely plausible; all invisible, automatic and anonymous....He has been rejected, not only by them but by himself."(*American Journal of Psychoanalysis*, 1949, 9:3)

The capacity for children to survive by molding themselves to the desires of their parents is surprising on the one hand and very understandable on the other. It is understandable because if children didn't become what their parents expected, they would be rejected emotionally and perhaps physically abandoned - they would not survive. On the other hand, the capacity they exhibit to unconsciously and consciously conform to the parents wishes is truly amazing. **You did exactly what you needed to do in order to survive and get as much love as possible from your family.**

THOUGHTS ABOUT PERSONALITY DIFFERENCES

Even children raised in the same family, though similar in many ways, are born with different genetic coding, unique capacities and experience their family in their own unique way. Look at the vast differences in personality between children in the same family. Ask your siblings how they experienced the quality of parenting which they received from your parents and you'll most likely be surprised at how differently from you they experienced your parents. While you may have experienced them as neglectful, they may have experienced them as nurturing.

Psychologists don't agree about whether or not your personality is primarily due to your genetics, experience in the womb, essence, environment or parenting. And they don't agree about the age at which your personality is formed. However, until recently the majority of authorities in the field of psychology believe that at birth your personality is "tabula rasa," a blank slate on which your personality is written (formed) very early in life (before the age of five). Now psychologists generally agree that genetics, experience in the womb, parenting and environment have the primary impact on the development and health of the personality. I concur with those psychologists that believe in addition to the above factors people are endowed with an essential self.

AGE OF FORMATION

Freud believed that the personality was formed by the age of five. Object Relations psychologists assert that personality is formed by the age of three. The psychiatrist Stanislov Grof claims that according to his research, personality is basically formed during the birth process. Other psychologists claim that their research shows that genes, at the point of conception, are the determining factor in personality development.

BIRTH ORDER

Some of these differences in children born to the same family are due to their birth order. Generally, more is expected from the firstborn child. So, they often take on adult responsibilities earlier and are more mature. The middle children often receive less attention than the oldest and youngest. The child born last is often spoiled and may be demanding and immature.

GENETICS

It is widely believed that some of the differences in how children experience the same parents is due to genetics. For example, some children's nervous systems are more sensitive than that of other children, so you might see one child raised by strict parents become a disciplined achiever while another child falls apart and drops out of society under the same amount of parental pressure. One thing is certain: *extreme parenting styles usually produce extreme behavior in their children.* In the example just described, strict parenting produced either an extremely disciplined child or an overwhelmed child, but *not* a balanced child.

Perhaps your personality type is due primarily to genetics. Psychologist Thomas Bouchard, a noted twin researcher, studied two identical twins (same genetics) who were separated at birth and reunited at the age of thirty-nine. Both had been married twice. Both were named James by their adoptive parents. Their personality and attitude profiles were very similar. Their likes and dislikes were similar. Their medical histories were similar. Both twins had slightly high blood pressure, and both had experienced what appeared to be a heart attack.

Many twins separated at birth have shown unusual degrees of similarities. Some of the twins, rejoined as adults, have the same phobias. One pair drink Budweiser beer and hold the bottle in the same manner, and one pair bite their nails at the same time.

Bouchard wrote, "If a personality were a symphony, nature contributes the score and nurture the orchestra." Psychologist David Lykken thinks that it is an endless circle which begins

145

with genetics. "Their genes have determined who they are, which in turn determines the kind of environment they'll seek and feedback they'll get, which in turn determines who they are." Clearly environment and genetics are both influential on our personality development.

But perhaps genetics are not as influential as twin researchers would lead us to believe. Identical twins frequently experience a "psychic" communication. They often report feeling each other's physical and/or emotional pain. Perhaps the similarities in choices and behavior experienced by identical twins after separation at birth are due to this "psychic" communication. Also, both twins experienced living in the same womb.

THEORIES OF TRADITIONAL ENNEAGRAM TEACHERS

Many teachers of the Enneagram believe that each of us enters the world with special capacities or "gifts." These gifts are what religions might call gifts from God. My explanation of how those gifts interact with our environment to determine the extent to which the gifts are distorted or fully expressed is explored in the examples which follow for Type Nine, the Peacemaker, and Type Eight, the Controller, personalities. For example, the gifts of a Type Nine personality are understanding and acceptance. Because children can't survive on their own and they don't yet have a sense of self, they tend to use their gifts to relate to the external world. So, the Type Nine is extra-accepting and understanding of its family. If the family notices the tendency of the Nine to be extra-understanding and accepting, they are likely to expect the Nine, more than their other children, to be a "good child," to "give in to them" and to "go along with what they are expected to do." Type Nine children "go along" and slowly lose touch with their capacity to accept and understand their own wants and needs. As adults, they are unconsciously sad and angry about their "self-abandonment" and keep giving in to others to avoid conflict and anger which may release their repressed anger and sadness.

Type Eight is another example. From infancy, the power and courage of Type Eight children are observable. They are generally considered to be defiant and difficult to control. This is an expression of their underlying gift of power, and at this level, self-protection (which often looks like defiance). One or both parents will respond to this child by trying to assert control; the child responds using its special gift of power by becoming tougher, more defiant and difficult to control. And, because the parents' excessive force seems unfair, Eights begin to feel justified in doing whatever is necessary to be powerful and control their own life. As adults, they aggressively control the people around them to protect their weak inner feelings. Instead of using their gift of power to assert their inner capacities and essence, they use it to protect an inner fear of feeling weak and vulnerable.

You can see how the gifts of the Nine, acceptance and understanding, can be lost in childhood. (Their biggest handicap, which is lack of self-understanding and self-acceptance, is paradoxically due to the fact that these gifts which helped them accept and understand their parents, but never blossomed into self-understanding and self-acceptance.) Likewise, the unique gifts of power and courage of the Type Eight became their biggest barrier to fulfillment. They began life being powerful and courageous and shifted their power and courage to protect themselves from feelings of weakness which would threaten to enter when their parents used excessive force. Their vulnerability and capacity to love easily got buried along with their feelings of being vulnerable.

OBJECT RELATIONS AND ESSENCE

The psychological theory of personality development on which this book is based is a relatively new psychological theory called Object Relations Theory in combination with the Theory of Essence. A very simplified introduction to personality based on Object Relations Theory and my conjecture about the emergence of essence as taught by Hameed Ali is included here.

As was noted in Chapter One, after you are born your first substantial contact with the world is usually your contact with your mother (primary caretaker). Although the umbilical cord is cut, your psychological connection continues. You are psychologically at one with your mother well before birth and for about five months after birth. The communication between you and your environment during this stage is direct and nonverbal. During this "Attachment Stage" of development you feel what your mother feels and vice versa.

From about six months to eighteen months, you are in the "Mirroring Stage" of development. Your essential strength is emerging and, at the beginning of this stage, you feel an urge to begin separating from your mother. During the remainder of the Mirroring Stage you develop your specific personality in a way which will protect you from physical and emotional pain, and get you the most love and support possible from your environment to help you develop a separate sense of who you are.

The final stage of development is the "Individuation Stage," which begins at about eighteen months and continues to the age of about three. During this stage, if there has been sufficient support and nurturing in the previous stages, the child realizes that it is a separate person and solidifies and refines its unique personality. By the age of three, its Enneagram personality type is well defined, and the child has lost most of its awareness of its essence.

According to the developmental psychologist Erik Erickson, trust is the first basic element established in the development of your personality. It lays the groundwork for later stages of personality development. The extent to which your environment is predictable, supportive and loving during the Attachment Stage, and while you were in the womb determines your general level of trust. It determines how thick and rigid your fixated personality shell becomes as you attempt to make yourself feel safe and protected from an uncertain or unsupportive environment. For example, if your environment during this stage of development is extremely overwhelming and threatening due to sexual abuse or psychotic parents, your shell may be so thick that you lose all contact with reality and become psychotic yourself.

To a great extent your level of psychological health, regardless of your specific personality type, is determined during the Attachment Stage. Your level of psychological health reflects the extent to which you can trust yourself and the world in which you live. It determines the extent to which you can accept reality as it is instead of how you expect it to be or how you try to see it in order to make yourself feel secure.

In Object Relations theory, the Mirroring Stage, from six to eighteen months of age, will be focused on more extensively because it is during this stage of development where the development of your personality type intensifies. This stage is where the discomfort and pain experienced by the child when its environment doesn't support the emergence of its essence leads to the formation of its specific Enneagram personality type. As mentioned earlier, the degree of rigidity or health which the specific personality type exhibits is determined by the level of trust established during the Attachment Stage.

In the Mirroring Stage mother acts as a "mirror" for the child. She provides the child with a picture (mirror) or reflection of who the child is. For example, if a two-year-old child falls, before it reacts it will look at mom (the mirror) to see how it should react. If Mom screams, the child screams. If she says "oops a booboo," the child will likely say "oops a booboo."

During the Mirroring Stage the separation process is beginning. What your specific personality type becomes depends on how accepting and supporting your mother and the rest of your childhood environment is of the emergence of your unique essential qualities such as strength and will. It depends on what feedback (mirroring) you are given about who you are. For example, if your mother doesn't want you to grow up and holds on to the view that you are an extension of her and that you will be mommy's little girl forever, you will either remain over-connected to her in some way and try to accommodate her or attempt to break away from her and try to take charge of your life.

Whatever aspect of essence that was attempting to emerge and that your human environment couldn't support or mirror healthily at this stage of your development becomes blocked and buried. You compensated for this repressed aspect of yourself by either trying to become *self-sufficient*, *accommodate* your parents or *take charge* of your life. Different personality types develop different fixated personality shells during the mirroring stage depending on their relationship with their mother (primary caretaker), their genetic inheritance, and which aspect of essence was most present at the end of the "Attachment Stage". Types Four, Five and Nine sought self-sufficiency, Types Two, Six and Seven tried to accommodate and Types One, Three and Eight tried to take charge.

SELF-SUFFICIENT TYPES
(TYPES FOUR, FIVE AND NINE)

The Self-sufficient Types were overwhelmed or ignored by their parent(s) and survived by emotionally withdrawing from them and ultimately trying to "not need" anyone. The image which they saw reflected in their parental mirror was that their essential needs weren't seen and would not be met.

Type Fours experienced a lack of support for their essential value during the mirroring stage and felt defective. They withdrew into a self-created inner world of eliteness, comforted themselves with their creativity and aesthetics, and tried to become *self-sufficient* by being different, creative and above needing other people.

The environment of the Type Five was too emotionally unpredictable and overwhelming due to too much involvement by the parents (invasiveness), confusing messages or an absence of emotional contact. They sought to become *self-sufficient* in their head, where they didn't have a need for relationships and comforted themselves with their precise and detailed thinking capabilities. They could think and observe in emotional safety in their head.

Type Nines, faced with a parental environment in which

they had to "fit in" and where conformity was needed, were unable to develop their essential will. They comforted themselves with their capacity to be supportive and understanding of others, and repressed their anger and inadvertently their lack of will. They dulled all of their feelings, especially angry feelings, and tried to become *self-sufficient* by not needing anything for themselves.

ACCOMMODATING TYPES
(TYPES TWO, SIX AND SEVEN)

The Accommodating Types never fully leave the Attachment Stage. They remain connected or dependent on their mother. When mother isn't available, they attach to someone else such as siblings, extended family, father, husband, wife or children. When they are attached, they accommodate the other person(s). As children, when they looked to their parents for mirroring they didn't see a reflection of their own being, they saw only their parents' needs because their parents didn't see them as separate and therefore couldn't be a mirror for them.

Twos comfort themselves with their capacity for compassion and love and *accommodate* other people to feel loved and needed. Sixes comfort themselves with their capacity to be loyal and *accommodate* others to feel secure. Sevens comfort themselves with their capacity for joy and *accommodate* others to support their childlike optimism and their pursuit of fun. Sevens tend to accommodate their extended family more than individuals. All three types accommodate other peoples' needs to keep them around and to feel supported and taken care of.

TAKE CHARGE TYPES
(TYPES ONE, THREE AND EIGHT)

Take charge types faced parent(s) who put a lot of pressure on them. They responded aggressively to the excessive pressure by either resisting or incorporating their parents demands and expectations. When they looked to their parents for mirroring, they didn't see themselves - they saw their parent's expectations to submit, achieve or seek excellence.

Type Ones were faced with criticism from parents who held unattainably high expectations for them. They comforted themselves with their high ideals and self-discipline and attempted to avoid the parental criticism by *taking charge* of their lives. Their way to take charge was to incorporate the unattainable parental expectations and develop an inner critic like that of their parents. By internalizing the parental critic they felt in charge of their life. They could "head off" criticism. No one had to tell them what to do because they were already doing what they were supposed to do.

The parents of the Type Eight were very controlling and many were physically abusive. The Type Eight felt threatened by this "unfair" attempt to control them. They comforted themselves with their power and courage and attempted to resist parental control and to protect their inner feeling of vulnerability by trying to *take charge* of and control their own life and the environment around them.

As a child, the Type Three personality was admired when they achieved and ignored when they failed. They comforted themselves with their capacity to perform and to avoid parental control. They tried to *take charge* of their life by incorporating their parents' dislike of failure and overvaluing achievement.

Our underlying essence seeks to emerge in each of us. However, its emergence was blocked early in childhood because the environment wasn't supportive enough. So instead, a substitute, defensive personality was formed in childhood to compensate for unsupported and blocked aspects of our essence. For the Heart Center Types (Types Two, Three and Four), the major blocked essential qualities are the feeling of being of value and feeling self-love. Fours substitute elitness and Twos substitute pleasing to compensate for blocked feelings of not being valued by their parents and not loved by themselves. Threes substitute achievement for the missing feeling that they had value. They need to earn value by achieving.

For the Head Center Types (Types Five, Six and Seven), inner peace is the major element of essence which was blocked in childhood. Trust is necessary to experience a sense of peace.

Fives substitute detailed thinking, and Sevens substitute planning to compensate for their lack of trust and inner peace. Sixes substitute skepticism to compensate for their lack of trust in themselves and their environment.

For the Gut Center Types (Types Eight, Nine and One), essential strength and will seem to be the major elements of essence which were blocked during childhood. Ones substitute self-criticism and Eights substitute aggressiveness to compensate for their lack of essential inner strength and power. Nines give into the will of others or become passive to compensate for their lack of essential inner will.

The sad fact is that the deficiencies or "holes" as A.H. Almaas, the author of several books on essence, calls them, cannot be filled in the way our personality is trying to fill them. That is why each type can never get enough eliteness, thinking, love, control or whatever it is that each is searching for. Each personality type is trying to fill a cup made out of desire which has a hole in the bottom.

So what can we do to feel whole and complete and move closer to a life of celebration? The suggestions for personal growth for your specific type are in Chapter 11. They are designed to help you begin to soften and refine your personality and make it more flexible and effective. As your personality softens and becomes more flexible, your essence will emerge to help you live a fuller, richer and more contented life.

To progress very far in personal growth, techniques which go beyond these recommendations for personal growth are needed. Techniques which are less familiar to most people, yet very powerful, are introduced in Chapter 15, including: meditation, emotional awareness, pursuing truth and presence. These techniques will help you develop a deeper understanding of your inner self and quiet your restless mind. Your mind holds your personality. As it becomes more quiet, your essence can emerge. Essence will be discussed more in Part Three.

CHILDHOODS OF SPECIFIC PERSONALITY TYPES

This section will help you understand your childhood better and learn how to be a better parent. It delves into specific styles of parenting experienced by different personality types to help you become more aware of the life-long impact of the way you were parented. Understanding how you were parented will increase your chance to break free and recover more aspects of your essence.

These insights are also presented to help you understand the impact which you have on your children so that you can be a better parent. If you ask your parents about how they were raised, you probably will discover that they were better parents to you than their parents were to them. There has been progress in understanding human behavior. You will most likely be better parents to your children then your parents were to you.

<u>CAUTION!</u> **THE EXAMPLES FOR THE CHILDHOOD OF EACH TYPE WHICH FOLLOW ARE JUST THAT: EXAMPLES!!!!!! JUST AS WE ARE ALL TRULY UNIQUE AS PEOPLE, THE ENNEAGRAM TYPES ARE SIMPLY PRESENTED AS AN EFFORT TO PROVIDE A SOUND BEGINNING IN YOUR JOURNEY TOWARD SELF- DISCOVERY. THE FOLLOWING DESCRIPTIONS OF CHILDHOOD EXPERIENCES ARE INTENDED TO HELP YOU BEGIN TO EXPLORE YOUR OWN UNIQUE CHILDHOOD.**

Even with the above caution, the majority of people don't feel that their childhood fits the exact descriptions which follow. And they don't exactly fit. Even if they did fit, it would be difficult for most people to be able to see the "fit" because they don't remember their childhood clearly and objectively.

Three reasons why the majority of people are usually unable to see their childhood clearly and objectively follow.

(1) Seeing our childhood clearly might cause us to re-evaluate our relationship with our parents and our whole perception of our life. We all desperately want to be loved and accepted by our parents. And most of us want to see our childhood as having been at least fairly good. Even if we weren't loved and accepted as a child, most of us will try to recall our childhood as if we were. On the other hand, some of us need to see our childhood as worse than it was. Either way, an objective and accurate view is unlikely. Reality is reality of the viewer in relation to their experience and background and their personality type.

(2) We develop our personality type early in childhood. Therefore, when we look back at our childhood we are looking through *eyes which have been limited in childhood by our personality type and have a limited capacity to see the whole picture.* For example, a divorce in early childhood is difficult for any child to experience. However, because of their personality type, a Type Three, Achiever personality may recall the divorce as a positive achievement because of how well (according to the Three's selective memory) the family handled it. A Type Four, the Artist, will likely see the same divorce as tragic (according to the Four's selective memory), and a Type Seven, the Optimist, will tend to view it as just another life event that works out for the best.

(3) The only parenting we really experience and know well is that which we receive from our own parents. So, whatever happened to us seems normal because it **was** the norm for us, and we didn't have anything else to compare it to. Children who were raised by parents who were strict generally see their parents as average or just slightly strict. I remember one client who felt his parents were average in their strictness, even though his description of his childhood included references to frequent severe beatings.

155

THE SELF-SUFFICIENT CHILDREN TYPES FOUR, FIVE AND NINE

The self-sufficient children discovered that the most comfortable way to get through their childhood was to withdraw and become self-sufficient. Fours withdrew into their own world of fantasies about their eliteness and nightmares about their feelings of defectiveness. Fives withdrew into emotionally disconnected, precise and detailed thinking. They stayed in their head where they couldn't be "touched" by the emotional world. Nines deadened their personal power to conform and retreated into daydreams. They went along with their parents' expectations, but they weren't fully there, weren't fully emotionally present.

EXAMPLE OF A TYPICAL TYPE FOUR (THE ARTIST) CHILDHOOD

Fours' relationship with their parent(s) usually felt good for the first few years of life. However, due to physical illness in the family, divorce, death or intensive career demands, their parent(s) became emotionally unavailable within the first few years of this child's life.

The message the Type Four child got from its parents became **"I am overwhelmed, leave me alone."** The Type Fours interpreted this parental message as, **"I am not acceptable to my parents. I am defective. To become acceptable I need to be unique and elite."**

So this child, who initially felt accepted, subsequently felt emotionally rejected. Unconsciously the child felt unwanted and abandoned. This child felt that the abandonment was due to its own defectiveness. It was filled with self-blame.

An adults we clearly see that this is frequently faulty logic. The parents usually left because of a personal crisis of their own. However, child development psychologists have demonstrated conclusively that early in life children feel that they are the center of the universe, and that they make things happen. When, for example, they walk, they think the moon is following them. When they cover their own eyes, they believe you can't see them. So it is perfectly reasonable for them to think that they caused their parent(s) to leave.

They go through life compensating for this feeling of being rejected and defective by developing their creativity and aesthetics. They strive to be special and elite. A Type Four related, "I was an only child and doted upon by my mother until I was about two years old. Then my parents got a divorce, and my grandmother developed cancer. I lived with my mother who, when she wasn't taking care of her mother, was tired and depressed. In a way, I lost both my mother and father at the age of two."

Another Type Four reported that her parents were divorced while her mother was pregnant. When she was born, and for several years after her birth, her mother was depressed. "I never felt wanted," she reported.

EXAMPLE OF A TYPICAL TYPE FIVE (THE THINKER) CHILDHOOD

The parental message experienced by the Type Five child was, **"I will emotionally overwhelm you, or I am emotionally unavailable."** Sometimes the overwhelming feelings from their parents came from over-involved (invasive) parent(s) who caused the Type Five child to retreat into its head. Other times parents of Type Five children were distant and emotionally unavailable, and the child's head (mind) became a retreat to avoid longing feelings for emotional contact. The child's response was to detach from their own emotions and begin to believe **"Emotions don't count. They interfere with thinking. I like to think and observe."**

Some of the Type Fives become so isolated from human interaction and into their head that they are disabled by strange and bizarre thoughts which they are afraid to share with anyone. Their potential gift of analytical thinking became a painful penalty. Others, with time, transform their inner, isolated thinking into profound, in-depth, breakthrough thoughts that they share with the world.

One Type Five related how unpredictable his parents were. The message he got from his parents was that he could do whatever he wanted, but, "Whatever I wanted to do," he said, "turned out to be wrong in their eyes."

EXAMPLE OF A TYPICAL TYPE NINE
(THE PEACEMAKER) CHILDHOOD

The parent(s) overlooked their child's needs and gave them the subtle yet powerful message, **"You must 'fit' into the family and do what we want you to."** They often remember good relationships with all parental figures and enjoyed stable childhoods because they gave into the wishes of their parents. Their response to the parental message was to believe, **"I like to FIT IN or do nothing."**

The conformity expected in the childhood of Nines was so powerful that they forgot themselves, over-adjusted to the desires of others and became helpless and impotent in knowing and satisfying their own needs. The only hope for a comfortable life was to understand and support what their parents wanted. In effect, as children, they lived through their parents. And, as parents they will likely live through their children.

As one Nine relates, his life was devoted to "making Mommy happy." To make her happy he needed to do what she wanted without question. He was a "good boy." And she, in return, was a "good Mom" and valued him. "When I make others feel OK, I feel of value, and then I'm OK."

Nines tend to adopt the desires of other people. In Enneagram terms, it's called coming in union with someone else. It's easy for Nines to get carried away by the enthusiasm or antagonism of other people. Nines desires were overlooked by their parents, and Nines as adults overlook their own desires. "I was taught to fit in and not cause trouble." Nines were in the background in the life of their parents. As adults, they feel comfortable being in the background with others.

THE ACCOMMODATING TYPES
TYPES TWO, SIX AND SEVEN

The Accommodating Types weren't provided the support and encouragement they needed to completely disconnect from their parents. Their parents' needs and feelings felt like they were their own feelings and needs. When their parents felt good, they felt good. When their parents felt bad, they felt bad.

Twos accommodated their parents because when their parents felt loved, they felt loved, and they felt their parents would take care of them. Sixes adapted by being loyal. If they were loyal and cautious, they felt that their parents would be loyal and take care of them and they would feel safe and secure. Sevens stayed in a state where if they uplifted Mommy and Daddy, they felt uplifted, and they wouldn't have to grow up. Mommy and Daddy would take care of them forever. And, of course, this style of relating with their parents carried over into all important relationships as adults.

EXAMPLE OF A TYPICAL TYPE TWO (THE PLEASER) CHILDHOOD

From early childhood, Type Two children are seen as sweet and giving. When they please they receive love and approval. They feel unwanted, unimportant, unneeded, and abandoned when they aren't able to make others "feel cared for." They repress their own needs and become very helpful and strive to be needed by their parents. They are often the "goodie two shoes" of the family. "I loved to tattle on my brother because then I was praised, and in my eyes that meant that I was a good girl," reported one Type Two.

The belief Type Two children develop early in childhood is **"I am loved and needed when I am helpful and please."** The message which they receive from one or both parents is **"Your love needs aren't important. Sense me, please me and take care of my need to feel loved."** These messages are verbalized as "I can't believe you're being so selfish," and communicated nonverbally as demanding stares or withdrawal of love when the Two isn't sweet and giving. The child receives parental love and attention when it supports the parents' need to feel loved.

Twos develop an unusually keen capacity to be aware of the emotional needs of one or both parents and focus most of their energy on meeting these emotional needs. To do this, they lose touch with their own needs. To avoid the fear of being abandoned, they need to fulfill their parents' emotional needs and to be viewed as good. One Type Two's father used to frequently say, "You want to make Daddy feel better and rub his back – I know you will because you are such a good girl!"

Many Twos become excessively needy due to early childhood abandonment as a result of the death, illness, or divorce of their parents. One Two explained that her need to be connected constantly was because she was an adopted child: "At night, my mother would lay me in my crib and sit with me until I was asleep. Quietly, she left the room, pausing at the door to look back. That's when she watched me climb out of my crib and follow her. To explain with accuracy why I didn't want my mother to leave me is impossible, but to hypothesize isn't. I've come to believe that it has to do with the fact that I was adopted. As a child I didn't understand why one day I was with "Mom" and the next I was in someone else's arms. All I could conceive was, I didn't want her to leave me too. Over the years, I chose to sleep on the floor next to my mom, no matter how hard or cold. As I grew older, I slept with my pet, and now I sleep with my fiance. Never could I have slept alone."

Other Twos become little Mothers or Fathers. One type Two's mother and father ignored her and their other children. She reported, "I needed someone to need me, and my brother needed a mother, so it satisfied both our needs. We've always been super close and will always be best friends."

One Two reported being a mother to her mother. "My mother married an American serviceman in Europe when she was sixteen and moved to this country. My father worked long hours. She was depressed and lonely. At a very early age I took it upon myself to comfort her and try to make her feel that someone loved her."

EXAMPLE OF A TYPICAL TYPE SIX
(THE LOYAL-SKEPTIC) CHILDHOOD

The parental messages experienced by the Type Six child are, **"Don't relax, be careful. People might unfairly judge you. You will never make it in this tough world."** The children's response to this message is to believe, **"I can protect** myself from an untrustworthy world by being vigilant, or I can confront my environment to reassure myself that I am safe."

These children feel unprotected, unsupported and fearful. Their parents' approach to discipline and general interaction with them is unpredictable and feels unfair to them. One Type Six reported that when she was very young, her mother divorced her father and left to find a guru. Her father was an airline pilot who was rarely at home. She felt like she couldn't trust anyone to be there for her.

Parents of Type Sixes consistently verbally or nonverbally warn their children that the world is dangerous. Type sixes as children are often belittled and told that they won't make it in life. Their vigilance and constant questioning about the motives of their parents and other people around them is an attempt to prevent unpredictable surprises. Questioning and worrying also keeps them away from the fearful feelings in their belly.

EXAMPLE OF A TYPICAL TYPE SEVEN (THE OPTIMIST) CHILDHOOD

The parental message to a Type Seven child is, **"Don't grow up. Make me happy, and I will take care of you."** Type Sevens avoided confronting painful problems as a child by making light of them. Their parents kept things light, wanted their children to have it all and wanted them to never grow up. The children learned to be charming, optimistic and planned fun things to do when pain or conflict threatened to enter their lives. Their response to this parenting was to develop the attitude, **"Don't worry, be happy, make others happy too."** As adults, being the optimists they are, regardless of how well or poorly they were really parented, they remember their childhood as happy. As one Seven wrote, "I loved my childhood and would relive it again if I had the chance."

The reason he became a Type Seven, reported one student, was because his parents fought a lot when he was young. "I told myself that if I was good, they would stop fighting. As I got older, this turned into changing the subject or telling jokes to stop the fighting."

THE TAKE CHARGE TYPES
TYPE ONE, THREE AND EIGHT

The Take Charge Types - One, Three and Eight - aren't accommodating nor self-sufficient. They try to take charge of their destiny, and they think that they do, even though, like all other types, they have developed a personality whose primary function is to cope with their early childhood environment.

Type Eights attempt to take charge by being in control of themselves and the people around them. Type Threes try to take charge by achieving so much that their parents will value them, and the Type Ones try to take charge by seeking unattainably high standards set by their parents. The parent(s) of all three of these types directly and intensively tried to run their lives. The parents of the Eights tried to overpower them. The parents of the Ones sought to make them always do more, do better and especially do things "right." The parents of the Threes wanted them to be successful so that they, the parents, could feel successful.

EXAMPLE OF A TYPICAL TYPE ONE
(THE PERFECTIONIST) CHILDHOOD

"You are not 'OK' unless you do important things the 'right' way, and you become the 'right' kind of person," is the parental message experienced by Type One children. In response, they develop the belief that **"I can't relax until every important thing I do is completed the 'RIGHT' way."**

As one Type One reported, "I couldn't ever relax as a child because the perfection that was expected of me was unachievable. Even my attempts at relaxation now, as an adult, are stressful. Because I can't 'waste' time, even my vacations must be efficient and 'useful'."

As children, Ones were highly controlled, often with narrow and strict rules enforced. Strict discipline or subtle guilt was used by their parents to make them obedient. Their parents or someone in their childhood environment created high expectations for them. One Type One said that her mother used to say, "Don't make any mistakes in life or you will become a failure like your sister."

As adults, Ones generally don't view the expectations of their parents as excessive because their own current demands on themselves are just as excessive. These children learn that they can never do enough to avoid criticism, punishment or judgment. They can and should always strive to improve and be "better." Due to such high expectations, they feel they have to behave more maturely than other children. They try to comply with these parental expectations but unconsciously resent having to try to live up to unattainable standards.

The parents of Type One personalities often directly or indirectly present unyielding and rigid beliefs about values, morals and behavior. For some Type Ones, the beliefs extend to every detail of life. "Both of my parents were very consistent and strict. Dad was raised a Roman Catholic and was very moralistic. He was very heavy into all of the 'should' and 'should nots.' I was his perfect little Princess and learned early on that I shouldn't disappoint him or I would hear about it. My mother believed, at least early on, that a regular routine was necessary and healthy. As an infant, I was fed every four hours no matter how much I cried. And she still takes great pride in the fact that I was potty trained by nine months."

Another Type One personality grew up in what she described as a "law and order" family. Her father was a deputy sheriff, and they went to church regularly. She couldn't recall being lectured about what she should do. However, she observed, "I suppose I understood that we were to behave in a certain way. Whether I understood or not, we were systematically and consistently taught to behave in specific, acceptable ways."

"I was raised in a family with a strong military tradition," reported another Type One. "I was sent off to a military school at the age of five, coming home for only one month a year until I was thirteen." Not all military school children are perfectionists, but strict military school training combined with parental attitudes which this man received prior to age five in a military family, would certainly lead to some extremes in behavior. Examples might be conformity or rebellion, or extreme strength or weakness.

EXAMPLE OF A TYPICAL TYPE THREE (THE ACHIEVER) CHILDHOOD

Type Three children are praised, rewarded, and talked about to others when they achieve and work hard. The downside is that they are ignored or punished when they do not achieve, leaving them feeling worthless or of little value when they aren't achieving.

Because these demanding parental expectations are too much for a child to bear, the result is that even as children Threes often feel "stressed for success," and turn to lying, bragging and false images of success to gain their parents' love. They try to "make" their parents feel like they are successful, and sometimes the "stressed-for-success stress" leads to a physical or emotional burnout.

The image sought by the Type Three child is **"I am productive, efficient and successful."** The parental messages are, **"Take care of my intense needs to achieve and be admired and respected. I will give you attention when you achieve."**

Their parents are, whether unknowingly or knowingly, using their children to satisfy their own need to feel successful. Threes are often raised by parent(s) who are, or who wanted to be, high achievers and need their children to be high achievers also. However, if the expectations are too high, the child may rebel or feel inadequate, insecure and become a "failure." If a Three isn't productive and successful, or at least can't appear to be successful, then he's nothing – a failure, and he'll feel worthless and depressed.

As one Three reported, "Both my parents were very successful and highly regarded in our town. I did well in sports, school, and became a very successful lawyer, yet I still push myself to achieve more. Looking back, I can understand why. All my parents talked about was their success, family achievement and the success of people we knew. They expected me to achieve. They were very busy all of the time and didn't give me much attention except when I came home a winner. I was praised and rewarded financially for every achievement."

EXAMPLE OF A TYPICAL TYPE EIGHT
(THE CONTROLLER) CHILDHOOD

The Eight children develop the belief, **"I've been unjustly treated. When I control myself and other people, I feel safe and powerful. Then, no one can mistreat me."** This stance is their attempt to achieve personal security in response to a strong parental message of, **"You better do what we want, or you will receive severe punishment."**

One or both parents are very powerful, controlling and sometimes physically abusive. "My father was a drill sergeant in the Marine corps. He raised me like I was a junior Marine," reported one Type Eight. *Or*, the parents were unusually "nice," smothering and invasive and used a sugarcoated, but subtle, powerful and unbendable style of control. "Everyone I know thought my mother was a happy, nice person. She was, if you did exactly what she wanted you to do. Otherwise, watch out."

As children, Eights stand up to what they perceive as unjust treatment. Because of what the child understood to be unjust treatment and the power they developed to cope with the powerful parent, they feel justified in reaching out and getting what they want. And they feel they can operate outside the rules of society. As a result, they usually are discipline problems in school, may fight with other children and commit criminal or other rebellious acts during their teenage years or even earlier.

So far in this book, I hope you have gained a sense of your specific personality type and how it was developed in childhood. In the next chapter, you will discover that each specific personality type tends to form intimate relations with other specific personality types. For example, Type Nines and Types Twos often marry.

CHAPTER
10

THE RIGHT PERSON FOR YOU

T he extent of love, compassion, truth, peace, strength and awareness which you experience in life depends on the depth and quality of your understanding and relationship with *YOURSELF*. When you understand, accept, appreciate and are intimate with yourself, you can experience more loving, more meaningful and more intimate relationships with others. Love enables one to know oneself.

The quality of inner love and outer love is the same. The more you love yourself, the more love you will be able to give to and receive from others. Most people are very confused about what love and intimacy are all about. In this chapter, "**being love**", "**deficiency love**", **intimacy**, and **Enneagram-based relationships** are explored.

Almost every person who has come to me for marriage counseling has placed most, if not all, of the blame for problems in their marriage on their partner and feels that they have tried the hardest to "make things work." They feel that if they can change their partner, the relationship will improve. **All problems in all marriages are created by both partners equally in magnitude but in their own particular way!** It's like two hands clapping. Which hand makes most of the sound? Half of the sound comes from one hand and half from the other.

They both have to change to produce a different sound.

I know what you're thinking to yourself right now! "That's probably true for most people. However, in my relationship, it **is** my partner's fault!" Well, even if the problems are all your partner's fault, which they aren't, you are still stuck because you **can't** change your partner. The only solution, in either case, is to change yourself.

Suggestions for personal growth are included in the next chapter on relationships If you really "get" the central message about love expressed in this chapter, you will understand that to get more love in life you need to love yourself more and become more psychologically healthy. You will shift your efforts from trying to "get" love and to change others and begin loving and nurturing yourself more. Then loving relationships will emerge as your love of yourself grows.

DEFICIENCY LOVE

The psychologist Abraham Maslow defined *deficiency love* as dependent, needy love. It is a major part of most loving relationships. It fosters co-dependent relationships. It is love which is sought to fill a deficiency or emptiness inside. The deficiency lover hopes that their wanting, desiring and needing will be ameliorated by their partner. They believe that what is missing in their life will be alleviated and their psychological pain lessened when they find the "right" person. The more internally deficient they are, the more needy and love-seeking they are.

It never works the way we hope. After we find the "right" person, the sugarcoating dissolves and the honeymoon is soon over. Except for some infrequent enjoyable periods, the inner pain, needing and wanting return. Partners in a deficiency relationship can never do enough or be enough to "make" their partner feel loved. Both partners are left with "love hunger."

The quality of the relationship is indicative of the inner quality of both partners. Therefore, people in deficiency love relationships will tolerate arguing which leads nowhere, emotional pain which is never resolved and sometimes physical abuse. Their fear is that they can't make it on their own and don't deserve better treatment. Their relationship with their parents probably had a similar quality to their current relationship. They probably have never seen or experienced a healthy relationship.

Deficiency love is possessive, jealous, stultifying, selfish, manipulative, pretentious and unrewarding. It is blind love. You have an imaginary vision of who your partner is and what the possibilities of the relationship are. The discomfort of deficiency love is part of all relationships. For many relationships, deficiency is actually the primary form of love they experience. The other end of the spectrum from deficiency love is being love.

BEING LOVE

Being love is the type of love which we all seek consciously or unconsciously. It goes hand in hand with healthy, loving relationships. It is the love of poems and stories with happy endings. It is love for the person's "being." It is non-possessive love, giving love. It is supportive love and based on mutual trust.

Being Love is welcomed into each partner's awareness, is intrinsically enjoyable and grows even better with time. It feels like an aesthetic experience. It is therapeutic, deep and rich, altruistic, intimate, allows for the autonomy of the other person, and it gives the partner a feeling of being worthy of love.

Being Lovers see their lover accurately and enjoy their similarities and prize their differences. They accept each other as they are. Forgiving each other comes naturally and effortlessly. The quarrels of Being Lovers are like summer storms: everything is fresh and more beautiful when the storm has passed.

As a person grows and develops, their experience of Being Love effortlessly and automatically increases. In addition to the general qualities of love which flower, the fragrance of the unique and special gifts of each of their Enneagram types are shared with their lover. The special gifts each type shares are: Type One shares their self-discipline and high ideals; Type Two shares love and compassion; Type Three shares their determination and capacity to perform; Type Four shares their aesthetic nature and creativity; Type Five shares wisdom and precision; Type Six shares loyalty and intuitive capacities; Type Seven shares joy and the ability to uplift; Type Eight shares power and courage; and Type Nine shares acceptance and the capacity to be supportive.

INTIMACY

The central aspects of your personality are developed out of the capacities you were born with and the quality of the intimate relationship which you experienced with your parents, especially as a baby and early in childhood. The intensity of your compelling desire, underlying fear, and lack of trust, are strongest when you're in a close, intimate relationship because the way you interacted with your parents in early childhood emerges as you become more open and trusting in an intimate relationship.

This is one of the reasons why healthy, longterm, intimate relationships are so difficult to maintain. The closer the relationship, the more intense the unique desires and fears of both personality types become. You need to be psychologically healthy to deal with the issues which arise; you need to know yourself and develop an intimate relationship with yourself to be able to establish intimate relationships with others.

Because an intimate relationship results from the depth of psychological sharing in a relationship, it involves trust and risk of rejection. As you become more intimate with yourself and your partner, both you and your relationship flourish. There is no end to the beauty.

SOME INSIGHTS INTO TYPICAL ENNEAGRAM INTIMATE RELATIONSHIPS

People constantly wonder who is the "right" person for them. Students of the Enneagram wonder which Enneagram type will lead to the best relationship.

Generally we are attracted to people who are similar to us; people who look similar to us and have like interests and values. We often marry people who are similar to one of our parents because we are used to that type of relationship, and it supports our self-image, even if we didn't get along with that parent. For example, the child of an alcoholic will often marry an alcoholic.

From the standpoint of your level of health as it relates to the quality of your relationships, two factors are most important; how psychologically healthy you are (psychological health is discussed in Chapter 13) and what aspects of your personality need to be supported or balanced by your partner (your co-dependency needs).

Your level of psychological health determines to what extent your relationship is based on **Deficiency Love** versus **Being Love**. What's important to remember is that your relationships don't produce your quality of being or level of health. They reflect your own internal level of psychological health.

Whether they are friends or lovers, people attract and are attracted to people of a similar level of psychological health. In most long-term relationships, each partner sees the other as the one with the problem. We all have problems, get confused and need support. However, your level of psychological health is approximately equal to that of your partner. Using an extreme example, people will argue with great certainty that the abused partner is healthier than the abuser. However, it is generally only unhealthy people who will tolerate abuse.

If you are an accommodating personality, due to your emotionally unhealthy personality type, you will more than likely be attracted to take charge or self sufficient personalities for intimate relationships. In this way, opposites attract as a way to seek balance in their life and to become whole. As Plato wrote, "Love is the pursuit of the whole." For example, Type Eight personalities take charge of relationships and are powerful and controlling, but are generally distant from feelings other than their anger. They often form relationships with Type Two, Four and Six personalities who are not very powerful or assertive, yet offer the Eight contact with softer emotions, and who tend to "give in" to the controlling nature of the Eight.

Ironically, the aspect of the other person which we were most attracted to when we first met is often the aspect that we like the least as the relationship progresses. If you were attracted to someone who was passive and easily controlled, eventually you will vehemently complain about their passivity. If you were attracted to a very controlling person, eventually you will vehemently complain about their controlling personality. Again, which hand produces the sound when two hands clap? They both contribute equally in magnitude but in their own unique way. Likewise, partners contribute equally to both successes and problems in a relationship.

Brief insights into typical relationships follow. The discussion emphasizes similarities and differences between the types.

TYPES ONE AND THREE

Types One and Three share a common need to work hard, produce and be efficient. However, the Type One seeks quality and substance in what they do, whereas the Type Three is more interested in immediate results, quantity and appearance. They are often willing to sacrifice quality.

There is good news and bad news about all relationships. One Type One married to a Type Three remarked about how exhausting their vacations were. "My husband wants to do so many things on a vacation, and I just want to do what we do efficiently and well. We both need a lot of time to rest after our vacations."

TYPES TWO AND NINE

Nines are out of touch with their own emotional needs. They are very habitual and predictable. Therefore, they provide Type Twos with an emotionally safe, stable and protective environment. They put the welfare of the Two before their own welfare. Twos are experts at sensing the needs of their partners. Twos draw out and take pride in the Nines potential for achievement and, more importantly for the Nines, Twos make them feel loved. Twos put the feelings of the Nine before their own feelings.

Such a co-dependence is a result of neither person being aware of their own needs. Both partners try to feel good by fulfilling the needs of the other. And both eventually feel upset that they've given themselves up in order to be loved by the other.

TYPES FIVE AND NINE

Fives and Nines both enjoy and feel comfortable with their partner having a need for private space. They both tend to like intellectual stimulation. A negative similarity is that their relationship may be emotionally dull and boring because both Fives and Nines are generally out of touch with their emotions.

TYPES SIX AND ONE

In a relationship with a Type One, Sixes find security in the black and white, well-defined beliefs of a One. The Ones are able to maintain their rigid beliefs with little sustained challenge from the loyal Six. They both are uncomfortable with uncertainty. Worrying and planning for a surprise-free and mistake-free future can form a common bond.

TYPES SEVEN AND THREE

Sevens can meet their need for adventure and have many options to keep them busy by relating to a Three. Threes are

173

busy achieving and generally have many projects going at the same time. Threes push for success can be supported by the optimistic mood of the Seven. Threes and Sevens aren't generally comfortable with confronting painful emotions. Sevens tend to have an idealistic view of family, and Threes often strive for the stereotypical ideal family. Threes often exaggerate their capacities and achievements, and the optimism of Sevens leads them to optimistically believe these exaggerations.

TYPES EIGHT AND FOUR

In addition to balancing strength and sensitivity in their relationship, Types Eight and Four both feel that they don't need to conform with the rules of society. This similarity of belief that they should make their own rules is a factor in their attraction. Many Fours and Eights are also similar because they like to "live on the edge," take risks and push their limits.

DIFFICULT INTIMATE RELATIONSHIPS

Some combinations of Enneagram types have difficulty maintaining long-term relationships. Generally, any two of the same personality types have difficulties in maintaining long-term intimate relationships. For example, many Eights are friends with other Eights. However, rarely are they married to each other for a very long period of time. They end up having a constant struggle for power. Even the giving, caring Twos like to be friends, but don't generally last in long-term, intimate relationships with other Type Twos. Two Type Twos in a longterm relationship tend to get enmeshed. One of them eventually feels emotionally overwhelmed or like they have lost their identity in the relationship. Rarely are lasting marriages seen between any of the same Enneagram types.

As with all generalities, there are exceptions. For example, Two Type Sevens reported having a healthy, long term marriage.

And I think that they did. On the Enneagram, the husband was a Seven and leaned toward his Eight Wing. The wife was a Seven and leaned toward her Six Wing. So, even though they were basically the same type, the extra power of the Seven husband leaning to the Eight Wing complemented the extra uncertainty of the Seven Wife who leaned toward the Six Wing.

ENNEAGRAM COMMUNICATION STYLES

COMMUNICATION STYLE FOR THE TAKE CHARGE, ACCOMMODATING AND SELF-SUFFICIENT TYPES

Your Enneagram personality type is expressed in how you dress, love, dream, work, communicate and in every aspect of your life. The communication styles of the **Take Charge** Types (Ones, Threes, and Eights), the **Accommodating** Types (Twos, Sixes and Sevens) and the **Self-sufficient** Types (Fours, Fives and Nines) are quite different.

In a relationship, **Take Charge** Types initiate and control the flow of events. They seek to take charge of people. **Accommodating** Types need to be around people. They tend to depend on others. **Self-Sufficient** Types tend to be interested in their own inner experience more than in other people and are indifferent to being around other people.

These three ways of relating can be observed in the distinctly different communication style of the three categories. For example, when **Take Charge** Types read a set of instructions to other people, their posture (non-verbal communication), tone, volume and speed of vocalization cause the receiver of the communication to feel like they are being *instructed* to do something. **Accommodating** Types would communicate the instructions as an *invitation* to do something. **Self-Sufficient** Types would communicate the same instructions in a slow, somewhat monotone voice, *sharing* what they are thinking while they are listening internally to what they are saying. By listening to how people speak you can learn valuable clues in determining their way of relating to others.

11

SUGGESTIONS FOR PERSONAL GROWTH

S elf awareness is the key to growth. For each Enneagram Personality Type I have developed three suggestions for growth and awareness. If you pursue these suggestions for personal growth appropriately, they will lead to self-improvement and improved relationships. The most powerful way to improve your relationships is to gain clarity and understanding about yourself. Intimacy in a relationship requires intimacy with yourself.

CAUTION! PEOPLE NORMALLY PURSUE SUGGESTIONS FOR GROWTH WITH THE ATTITUDE THAT THEY SHOULD CHANGE THEMSELVES OR SOME ASPECT OF THEIR LIFE IMMEDIATELY. THEY REJECT WHO THEY ARE PRESENTLY AND TRY TO FORCE THEMSELVES TO BECOME BETTER OR DIFFERENT. HOWEVER, AS WILL BE MADE CLEAR IN THE SECTION ON TRUTH IN PART THREE OF THIS BOOK, THAT BELIEF CAN ACTUALLY LESSEN AND DISTORT PERSONAL GROWTH. I WAS EVEN RETICENT TO INCLUDE THESE RECOMMENDATIONS IN THE BOOK BECAUSE OF THIS DANGER.

However, if you pursue these suggestions with the attitude that you want to experiment with them and explore them to see how they influence your life, and if you do it with compassion for yourself and with the goal of discovering greater clarity and truth about yourself, they can be extremely helpful to you. Only then will they become tools for self-observation and self-understanding, which are the basis for meaningful and lasting growth.

Part Three of this book focuses in more detail on tools for self-observation and heightening inner awareness. *Self-observation, leading to a heightened awareness and understanding of your desires and fears, will automatically lead to growth and is the single most powerful method.*

Desires and fears are like two sides of a coin. One does not exist without the other. Much of our confusion and pain in life is because we only see the desire side of the coin. For example, Type Threes are very aware of and proud of their desire for success. However, most of them completely block out the flip side of the coin that the desire for success is driven by the fear of failure and fear of rejection. Without this recognition, they are stuck in a search for glory which is only superficially rewarding. Their biggest rewards come from hope and dreams of future achievement. However, when they do achieve, they are only temporarily satisfied and are driven to begin hoping for something in the future all over again. Their fear of failure and rejection is still within them

The primary way out of this never-ending circle is to become aware of both sides of the coin. When Threes fully understand that their childhood-based fear of failure, one side of the coin is fueling their desire for success, the other side of the coin, they automatically begin to relax (a scary word to a Type Three), reduce the intensity of their desire to succeed, and begin to fulfill their deeper needs. They become more aware of their deep need for love, meaning and freedom, which were overlooked in childhood and they understand that these needs can't be attained by focusing all their efforts exclusively on achieving.

Self-observation and awareness are the general keys to freedom. What you have already discovered about yourself combined with trying the exercises in Chapter Fifteen will help you expand your awareness of yourself. This self-awareness automatically leads to growth. To continue the awareness process, three suggestions for growth for each Enneagram type are as follows:

TYPE ONE

1. Type Ones, more than any other type, are driven by the inner critic and the demon "should." Changing the intensity of your expectation to be perfect can be helped by mentally changing your expectations expressed as "shoulds" to "prefers." The anger and feeling of being overwhelmed by "terrible" mistakes can be reduced by labeling mistakes as "unfortunate" rather than "terrible." Reducing the intensity of the emotional reactions which are triggered by these "irrational labels" and making them more "rational" increases your clarity, softens your inner critic and actually improves your efficiency and productivity.

2. Be patient with your own capacity to avoid making mistakes and that of others around you. Don't let your inner critic rule your life and attempt to rule the lives of those around you. Learn to soften the judgment which you internalized as a child.

3. Use your self-righteous anger as a signal or trigger to help you become aware of the anger in you which is generated by your perfectionistic expectations. Relax, take a few deep breaths and remind yourself that this self-righteous anger is one of the main barriers to getting what you really want in life.

TYPE TWO

1. Your excessive pride needs to be softened by the humility which comes with recognizing your own faults and needs. Be willing to ask other people for help.

2. Realize that when you please and give too much, you get over-tired and feel used. It is possible to please and, at the same time, honor your own need for rest and support. By striving to

please only when it is "your pleasure," and expecting nothing in return, you learn to balance your desire to please with with your need to take care of yourself. Your relationships will become more **mutually** nourishing.

3. Increase your awareness about your tendencies to be possessive and to manipulate people into needing you. Become more openly direct about your needs. Manipulation and possessiveness ultimately undermine your capacity to form the loving and committed relationships which you seek.

TYPE THREE

1. Resist the temptation to sell out to the image you believe your family and society holds of you in order to feel admired and accepted. Learn to trust, tune into, and respond to your own feelings. Only then will you need less admiration from others and find deeper and more lasting internal satisfaction.

2. Honor your body. Realize that to live a **long** and **productive** life your body needs to be kept healthy.

3. Recognize that your world will not collapse if you set a more reasonable pace for your work and include rest breaks in your schedule. In fact, slowing down tends to reduce the chance of making mistakes and gives you a chance to make better decisions. Realize that the self-doubt which you feel when you relax is due to a change in your personality which occurs when you shift to the Six Point on the Enneagram. It is a temporary change within you. You can rest assured that your capacity to achieve does not change.

TYPE FOUR

1. Realize that the extra good feelings which come from striving to be unique and elite sets into motion a pendulum which at any moment can swing to extra depressing and angry feelings. You can reduce your mood swings by softening your tendency to strive to be elite.

2. Understand that your hypersensitivity to the remarks of

others leads to anger and depression. Practice taking the remarks of others less personally. Realize that their remarks are a result of the views of their personality type and are not likely to be an accurate assessment of you.

3. Become more aware of your psychological boundaries – where you end and others begin. Realize that other people's feelings can "penetrate" your boundaries without your awareness. Practice becoming aware of whose feelings are whose when you are around other people.

TYPE FIVE

1. Your avoidance of emotions and reliance on thinking tend to restrict your capacity to interact with others and can isolate you from reality. Sensing your body will connect you more with your emotions and broaden your understanding of yourself and your relationships with other people.

2. Realize that being cooperative with others is not a sign of losing. Delay judging other people and use some tact in addition to facts to influence those you care about.

3. Utilize your well-developed capacity to understand the world in order to understand your whole self better, including your emotions, intuition and relationships. Socrates, who was a Type Five personality, stated, "Know thyself." Knowing yourself relates to directly sensing inner awareness more than thinking analytically.

TYPE SIX

1. Recognize that anxiety underlies all human emotions. Don't unnecessarily increase your level of fear by being anxious and afraid because you, as a Type Six, sense your anxiety more than other people. Their anxiety may be the same or greater than yours, but they may not show it or feel it because they are less in touch with it.

2. Develop a trusting relationship with at least one person with whom you can discuss your fears, and who can help you

put them into a reasonable perspective. Forming one trusting relationship will help you develop more trust in yourself and others.

3. Try not to overreact to authority figures by being over-submissive or over-rebellious. Try to see them as they are, just other human beings doing their job in the best way their personality type allows. However, if you are being mistreated, experiment with standing up for your rights.

TYPE SEVEN

1. Tolerate your boredom and pain more. Slow down, stay with projects and people a little longer. Even when someone interferes with your plans for fun, causing your reactionary anger, blaming and criticism to erupt, try to pause, slow down to see what is really happening and try to gain clarity about your role in the situation.

2. Be aware that your tendency to be over-optimistic and over-enthusiastic can result in ignoring danger and loss of self-control. You will be less likely to exhaust yourself and less likely to take excessive risks in life.

3. When seeking friends, look for quality in people in addition to quantity. Look for emotional depth in people in addition to how funny and exciting they are.

TYPE EIGHT

1. Allow yourself to feel your vulnerability by admitting mistakes and weaknesses. Realize that aggression and strength are not the same. Strength provides you with the energy to be in the world in a comfortable and personally satisfying way, and to discover the truth about yourself. Aggression is an angry, defensive reaction against the fear of feeling weak and being controlled. It satisfies your compelling desire but keeps you from satisfying your deep need for a close relationship.

2. Realize that getting back may feel like the right thing to do, but that it is only a weak reflex reaction which is an attempt to make yourself feel safe. It will waste your energy, deplete

your strength and reduce your capacity to be in control of your life.

3. Be strong enough to understand that your controlling and power-based approach to life is the result of fear generated by a severe, unfair, and controlling elements in your childhood environment. As an adult, most of your controlling and confrontation is to protect yourself and to reassure yourself that you are not weak and that no one will ever unfairly control you again. Use this awareness to access your compassion and be just and fair in your treatment of others as well as yourself.

TYPE NINE

1. When you reach for food, liquor, the television or any other numbing agent, recognize that you are most likely escaping from anger and conflict. Instead, try to face anger and conflict directly. Work to discover the source of your anger and deal with it. Your anger won't build up and you won't have to numb yourself as much as usual.

2. Realize that being good or compliant as a way of showing love doesn't represent mature love. Love for you will become more real when you can let go of the fear of a conflict and become more open with those you love. Saying no lays the groundwork for a big yes in love as well as life. At a more subtle level, especially for union sub-types of the Type Nine, saying no to someone else feels like you are saying no to yourself. Get clear, be powerful and more alive by saying NO and make room for a big YES!

3. Recognize that you have essentially lost contact with your own will. You have been begrudgingly using your power almost exclusively in the service of others. Become more aware of your own needs and assert your own willpower. Experiment with new styles of dress, new ways to work and love. Develop aspects of life which are enriching and rewarding to you.

Part Three of this book focuses on general techniques for growth and transformation instead of specific recommendations for growth.

PART 3

LOOKING INWARD

PART THREE
LOOKING INWARD

A police officer noticed a man crawling on his hands and knees under a lamppost. He was apparently searching for something. When the officer questioned the man about his behavior, the man said he was searching for the key to his safe, which contained his most precious possessions. The police officer searched the area with the man for awhile and then the officer decided to become more systematic about the search. He asked the man where and when he had lost the key. To the officer's surprise, the man said he'd lost the key somewhere in his house many years ago. He explained that he was searching outside of his house under the lamppost because it was easier to search where there was light. He hadn't paid his electrical bill and his electricity had been shut off, so there was no light in his house.

This modern version of an ancient story exemplifies how, due to our illusions, we are searching outside of ourselves for the key to that which is true, real or substantial. As you become more aware of who you are and how you got to be the way you are, you will become increasingly clear about how essential qualities were lost or buried inside of you many years ago in early childhood and that you have been looking for the key to reclaiming them outside of yourself – in relationships, jobs and activities instead of looking inward to your essential reality for the key to aspects of your essence such as love, compassion, truth, peace, strength and awareness.

The process of transformation is challenging and liberating. The truth about ourselves involves a constant search, effort and desire for a deeper and truer understanding of our personality, inner nature and the human condition.

Outside there is a lot of light, and the search seems easy. However, even though searching in your inner darkness seems slower and more difficult, that is where the key lies. The key to understanding your personality, your inner nature, and the human condition, lies inside. How to delve into your inner nature is discussed in Chapter 15.

As a child you need to focus your attentions outside, toward your parents, because your life depends upon them for nurturance and support. As you mature and grow, your awareness and energy will slowly shift its center from the outside to the inside, where the key to joy, peace and contentment lies. But most people resist moving inward and spend most of their time searching outwardly for that which lies within. Out of necessity, early in life you looked to your parents, but now, as an adult, you continue to look outward to relationships, possessions and work instead of inward.

Psychotherapy is based on looking inward in the present moment. If, for example, you visit a psychotherapist and share how explosively angry you became when your friend ignored you last week, the therapist will gently guide you inward into the present moment to help you understand how this temper explosion relates to your personality and the motives, fears and feelings which underlie your personality. You will be helped to understand that how you reacted to your friend is similar to how you relate to your spouse, which is similar to how you related to your parents, which is similar to how you are relating to the therapist right now in the therapist's office.

The therapist will help you become aware of your feelings in the moment, how these feelings are felt in your body now, and how, as you face and explore your feelings now, you can gain new understanding about your unconscious fears and desires. The therapist will help you understand that when your friend ignored you, on a unconscious level you were reminded of how, as a child, it seemed that your parents were ignoring you, and how anger pent up from your childhood was released and directed against your friend. As you face and experience your inner anger with the help of the therapist, your inner anger will begin to dissolve and you will feel better and relate better.

In other words, the therapist will take you inward to your present feelings and memories of childhood to help relieve pent up anger from childhood and help you look outward to understand the situation with your friend and other similar situations in your life.

If the therapist didn't guide you inward, but instead just discussed the anger which arose when your friend ignored you, your growth in understanding and the resolution of anger in your life would have been much less in comparison to what you could have attained by looking inward.

You will notice as you work with your personality issues using the Enneagram and grow in understanding of the Transformation process, your attention shifts inward and to the present moment. And, paradoxically, the light of understanding which will be shed on your inner darkness will also illuminate your outer life. Your relationships, your work, and everything you do in life will become more enjoyable, and rewarding through this new understanding and awareness. You will be able to answer with greater clarity the questions posed at the beginning of this book. And your journey toward freeing yourself, being whole and living your full human potential will be supported by this inner growth and development. It will unify the inner and outer and every aspect of your being.

Part One of this book gave you a quick overview of the Enneagram and personality. Part Two, which went into more depth about the Enneagram and introduced relations between Enneagram types, was more extensive and included recommendations to take a workshop or meet with a couple of friends who are the same Enneagram personality type as yourself. To deepen and integrate this material takes a lot of time and commitment and usually requires the aid of a psychotherapist or a supportive environment.

In Part Three, Chapter Twelve presents the concept of personal transformation and outlines the twelve levels of the transformation process. Chapter Thirteen is designed to help you determine your own level of development, and Chapter Fourteen alerts you to some of the obstacles to transformation.

Paradoxically, Chapter Fifteen, which delineates practices such as meditation is designed to help you "delve" inward, is fairly short, even though "delving" inward toward your essence is the most challenging and rewarding adventure which you can undertake. To understand the power of these practices and to faithfully practice them consistently and effectively requires a major commitment to your personal transformation.

*   *   *

A prominent psychologist went to a wise teacher seeking the wisdom of the ages. He had traveled a long way and was full of questions. The teacher ignored the psychologist's eager questions and offered him tea instead. The teacher was enjoying the tea. The psychologist was getting angry.

The teacher offered more tea. As the psychologist impatiently waited for "the wisdom," his teacup was filling. Then the tea overflowed into the saucer. And then, to the psychologist's chagrin, the tea began to overflow onto the floor. The psychologist protested, "Stop, can't you see what you are doing. You are making a mess and wasting time. Answer my questions!"

The teacher explained, "Your mind is overflowing with thoughts, ideas and knowledge. Before you can receive wisdom, you must go back home and empty your mind of thoughts so that wisdom can enter."

Most people's minds are overflowing with thoughts, and images from childhood that interfere with their capacity to see themselves clearly and the world as it really is. What you discover as you slow down and quiet your mind is that you become open to the present wisdom of innate intelligence. You can't learn about yourself from books alone. If you memorize some facts from books, you are borrowing someone's knowledge. This knowledge often conflicts with other borrowed knowledge and may simply occupy your mind. It can't become wisdom until it becomes a part of your experience, a part of your being. Part Three contains less specific knowledge and instead encourages you to open to inner wisdom by practicing the awareness exercises. These exercises will provide you with an initial insight into transformation practices. These exercises are windows to your inner world.

The information in Part Three points the way inward to release more of your essence. To gain greater depth, the help of a transformation teacher or psychotherapist trained in these approaches is usually necessary to support your efforts and to guide your journey.

TRANSFORMATION

WHAT YOU CAN EXPECT
AS YOU GROW

T he concept of psychological growth is familiar to most people. It is based primarily on increased awareness and understanding of your childhood, personality, emotions and relationships. The purpose of psychological growth, as Freud expressed it, is to enable you to improve your personality so you can work and relate more effectively.

Even though developing a healthier personality is important and can speed the process of transformation, it is only part of the transformation process. The process of transformation also involves a fundamental change in who you think you are. During the process of transformation you become more and more aware that you are not just your personality. You realize that at the deepest level you are your essence. That special something that makes you who you really are. As you transform you become more and more identified with your essence and less identified with your personality. You move inward, closer and closer to the core of your being, to experience the aspects of your essence such as love, compassion, trust, and understanding.

Almost everyone enjoys watching and interacting with infants and young children. The sparkle in their eyes and

193

expression of love and acceptance is heartwarming and beautiful. Infants are innocent, spontaneous, joyous and curious. It is amazing how quickly this vitality is constricted and lost. Out of necessity, their aliveness and sparkle is reduced dramatically by the age three and even more by the age of seven, so that they can adapt to their family and environment.

Their aliveness is not lost! Instead, it is constricted and buried beneath psychological defense mechanisms which block painful feelings of anxiety and frustration. Their aliveness is enclosed in a fixated personality shell which attempts to help it get love and survive in the world. Your essence is this precious, sparkling aliveness.

The good news is that your essence is not completely buried inside your fixated personality shell. You experience it occasionally when watching a sunset, walking in nature, playing with a child, making love or "in the flow" while playing a sport, dancing or playing music. It is during these moments when you experience life as beautiful, harmonious, tranquil and joyful. You are relaxed yet alert and life requires no effort.

As an adult, you have capacities, knowledge and skills which can support your survival in the world. With these capacities you can begin work on the transformation process. You can release and develop your essence. The innocence and love of your essence is expressed through your adult understandings and capabilities. As you learn to support the emergence of your essence, your inner beauty, radiance, love compassion, truth, strength, power, awareness, courage, intelligence, peace and joy unfold. You become more at ease with yourself and the world.

To help you get a feel for what happens as you turn your attention inward and progress in your transformation, twelve levels of transformation are outlined and then briefly discussed.

TWELVE LEVELS OF TRANSFORMATION

Because everyone's personality is unique and yet similar to others, the transformation process for everyone is unique and yet similar. The **Twelve Levels of Transformation** I have outlined are designed to provide you with a *general* feel for the transformation process.

The growth needed to be achieved at Levels One through Three begins with thoroughly understanding your Enneagram personality type, as discussed in Parts One and Two of this book.

Levels Four through Nine are more associated with *transformation*, a major change in the understanding, acceptance, experience and expression of who you are, and the emotional issues underlying how you got to be who you are. These levels involve the shift of your identity from your **personality** to **essence**. They involve developing clarity about the reality of the connection between your innermost self and what you experience in the world.

Levels Ten through Twelve involve an even greater shift from identifying with you personality to centering yourself in your essence.

The fact that something more exists in our life than simply our body, mind, and emotions, was alluded to by the Nobel Prize-winning brain researcher John Eccles, when he said, "I go all the way with my fellow scientists in understanding the brain physically. But it doesn't explain me, or human choice, delight, courage, or compassion. I think we must go beyond...., There is something apart from all the electricity and chemistry we can measure."

The "something more" referred to by John Eccles is your essence. An analogy consisting of a limousine, driver and passenger can be helpful in understanding the various aspects of yourself such as your body and personality (mind and emotions) as they relate to your essence. The body of the limousine is symbolic of your physical body. The engine is symbolic of your emotions, your energy of motion. The chauffeur is symbolic of your mind. The passenger is symbolic of your essence. Normally you are identified with your body, mind and emotions. Your essence is ignored. It is in the back seat. As you become more transformed, your essence becomes more and more important in relation to your body (limousine), emotions (engine) or your chauffeur (mind). You no longer ignore your essence. It becomes the guiding force for your body, mind and emotions.

The transformation experience referred to in levels Ten through Twelve is not easy to define. Words are not adequate to discuss what happens at these levels. The concept of transformation at these levels becomes fully meaningful only after you begin to directly experience your essence. Your personality softens and relaxes. It loosens its constraints on your essence and begins to seem more like the fragrance of your deepest essence than the mechanical, robotic habits.

Your focus shifts from just softening your fixated personality shell and reducing the intensity of your desires to delving deeply into yourself, and from just getting along in life to living a life of celebration which is more meaningful, joyful and spontaneous.

TWELVE LEVELS OF TRANSFORMATION

The twelve levels of transformation presented here describe what awaits you as you become more self-aware committed to your essence, travel the path of personal transformation and what you need to do to progress along the path.

DISCOVER YOUR PERSONALITY

1. Discover the primary underlying motive for your personality

2. Understand how your personality was developed

3. Appreciate your personality

BECOME CENTERED IN THE HERE AND NOW

4. Practice being present here and now

5. Develop a self-observation practice

6. See through your own eyes - act, don't react

CLARIFY AND DEEPEN YOUR RELATIONSHIPS WITH YOUR FAMILY AND FRIENDS

7. Acknowledge the mirror quality of others

8. Awaken your compassion and your ability to help others

9. Be real, open, and authentic

OPEN TO THE GROUND OF YOUR BEING BY SOFTENING YOUR PERSONALITY AND DISCOVERING WHAT IS YOUR OWN: UNCONDITIONAL LOVE, TRUTH, AND MEANING

10. Come from spaciousness and emptiness

11. Witness from the heart and break the illusion of separateness

12. Celebrate all of life and simply allow life to happen

AS INFORMATION IS INTRODUCED ABOUT LIFE AT LEVELS OF TRANSFORMATION WHICH ARE DISTANT FROM YOUR PRESENT PERSONAL EXPERIENCE, MISINTERPRETATIONS, FEAR AND UNINFORMED JUDGMENTS USUALLY ARISE — AND THAT'S NORMAL — IN PSYCHOLOGY IT IS CALLED RESISTANCE TO UNDERSTANDING THINGS YOU MAY NOT BE COMPLETELY READY TO ACCEPT — SO, TRY TO READ WITH AN OPEN MIND AND HEART — WHEN YOU ARE READY, THIS MATERIAL WILL BECOME MORE IMPORTANT AND CLEAR TO YOU — DON'T ACCEPT ANYTHING PREMATURELY — WAIT UNTIL IT RESONATES WITH WHO YOU ARE.

Everyone, at some point in their life, has at least briefly experienced a transcendental state, or as Abraham Maslow called them, peak states. It may have been while you were hiking in the forest, giving birth to a baby, sharing an intimate time with a friend or in innumerable other ways. The feeling of being at ease, feeling whole, peaceful and accepting are part of the transcendental state. As you progress in your personal transformation, you inevitably become more in tune with these feelings, which you previously experienced by chance. You feel like you are coming home to your true self.

In the next chapter, you will gain better insight into your current level of mental health for your specific personality type. This will help you understand more clearly where you are now in the process of transformation.

LEVELS OF PSYCHOLOGICAL HEALTH

G eorge Gurdjieff taught that the balance of relatively healthy essence and a "personality that is not crushingly heavy" is necessary for healthy development. In general, your development progresses as you break free from your fixated personality shell.

People within each Enneagram personality type function at different levels of psychological health. Before techniques are introduced to help you grow and transform, five levels of psychological health will be discussed to help you determine at what level of health you are currently functioning, and what you can expect to experience at higher levels of health as you continue your process of growth and transformation.

Generally, just as we have a personality type which is home base (where we are most of the time), we have a level of psychological health which is also home base. For periods of time we may feel much better or much worse. However, we are generally functioning most of the time at one level of psychological health. Five levels of psychological health will be presented: **psychotic, dysfunctional, normal, healthy, and free.**

The term psychological health refers to your ability to care for yourself and others, to be contented and to work productively. It is used in this chapter to help you understand your level of psychological development. I use this term with great reservation because people tend to judge themselves and/or others harshly about their level of psychological health. Whether you are dysfunctional, normal or healthy does not reflect the quality of your efforts to grow psychologically. It usually reflects the degree to which your early childhood experiences supported or restricted your capacity to develop your personal potential.

If you are **psychotic**, your lack of contact with reality may be so severe that you live in a world of hallucinations and delusions. You may need the help of medication and/or hospitalization to live from day to day. An example of the psychotic level is schizophrenia.

When you are **dysfunctional**, you are in such psychological pain and so out of contact with reality that it's difficult to maintain healthy relationships or be productive in the work place. Someone who experiences panic attacks and has difficulty leaving the security of their home is an example of the dysfunctional level of health.

When you are **normal**, you are like the norm or average person's psychological health. You are still hurting, trapped by the desires of your personality, and yet you feel like this is all you can expect from life. You function in the world, but you don't generally feel comfortable or satisfied. Even at this level, you may need medication to help cope with migraine headaches, anxiety or other symptoms of psychological discomfort.

The great majority of people don't attain a **healthy** level of psychological health, and it is not considered to be the highest level of development. At the healthy level, you are still strongly connected with your personality type as described by the Enneagram. You are very aware of and comfortable with your self and can interact with others well. If giving is used as an example, a dysfunctional Two would give to manipulate. Normal Twos might drain themselves by giving too much. For healthy Twos, the pleasure of giving would come from the act of giving itself, not from obtaining something through manipulative giving. Their giving would enliven them, not drain them.

The **free** level of health, where you are free of your fixated personality shell and express your essence, is the most difficult level to attain and describe. In fact, it almost defies description. You need to experience it to fully understand it. Describing personality types was easy by comparison, because personality types are narrow, fixated and familiar to us. The characteristics of essence which emerge at the free level as a result of the transformation process are unfamiliar, broad rather than narrow, flexible and fluid rather than fixed.

Breaking free of the desires of the personality at this level leads to a state of wholeness, contentment, presence, truth, love and freedom. Living becomes a process rather than a fixated set of habits. Our truest, deepest self becomes the source for our moment-to-moment awareness of life.

One way to understand the free level of health is to examine what happens as we move away from it to healthy, then normal, then dysfunctional and finally to psychotic levels of health. Descending into less healthy levels of health leads to less freedom, flexibility and awareness in life. For example, life at the dysfunctional level is painful, limited and fearful. Life at the psychotic level is trapped in a dreamlike world of hallucinations and delusions, out of touch with reality. Conversely, moving toward higher levels of health from psychosis, to dysfunctional, to normalcy, to healthy, to free, leads to more and more joy, peace, and meaning in life.

Likewise, people who learn to live more and more from their essence at the free level not only retain basically the same physical body, they retain the same personality type. However, both the level of health of your personality type and your physical body affect your efforts to transform immensely. A dysfunctional personality type, like a dysfunctional physical body, interferes with your ability to attain and live a more healthy life, whereas having a healthy body and well-developed personality enhance your ability to actualize your deeper, more meaningful and essential needs and wishes. A healthy body and well-developed personality act as vehicles for your essence rather than obstacles.

The Enneagram teaches us that the ultimate state of psychological health is the capacity to freely express the highest potential of all nine personality types (nine aspects of essence). Freedom is achieved when the capacities of each personality type are readily available to you. They assume their natural place in the totality of your being. This allows you to respond to situations as they are, not as you hope they are or want them to be. The aspects of your personality necessary to respond to any situation arise spontaneously and effortlessly as you need them. You become balanced, at ease, fluid and flexible and able to creatively interact with your inner-self and the outer world. You feel as if your individual identity is merged with all of reality.

This ultimate state is not some exotic state. It is nothing other than being yourself in the moment, free from over-reliance on your compelling desire and free from the fixations in your personality which were established in childhood. You don't lose anything real, you only lose the false aspects of your personality and your false perceptions of life. When you step out from within the fixated aspects of your personality, life becomes free, exquisite, meaningful, adventurous and loving; a true celebration.

LEVELS OF HEALTH

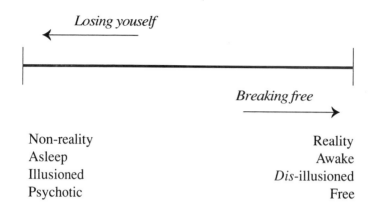

Losing youself

Non-reality
Asleep
Illusioned
Psychotic

Breaking free

Reality
Awake
Dis-illusioned
Free

Dysfunctional	Normal	Healthy
Compulsive/Impulsive	Habitual	Flexible
Dependent	Dependent/ Interdependent	Interdependent
Destructive	Destructive/ Constructive	Constructive
Overwhelmed	Hurting	Comfortable
Never Enough (Neurotic Needs)	Somewhat Satisfied	Often Satisfied
Serious Interpersonal Conflict	Interpersonal Conflict	Interpersonally Comfortable
Controlled by environment	Controls the environment	Flows with the the environment

LEVELS OF PSYCHOLOGICAL HEALTH AND THE ENNEAGRAM

A thumbnail sketch of levels of health for each personality type follows to give you a "feel" for dysfunctional, normal, and healthy characteristics for each state. A "feeling" for how these personality types tie into selected portions of the Diagnostic and Statistical Manual of Mental Disorders (DSM III-R) is also included. The DSM III-R is the manual used by psychotherapists to understand their clients.

Please remember that the outline which follows is intended to provide a rough sketch and brief overview of levels of health as they relate to the Enneagram.

Type	Dysfunctional	Normal	Healthy
One Perfectionist	Intolerant	Judgmental	Tolerant
Two Pleaser	Needy Manipulator	Insecure Pleaser	Nurturing
Three Achiever	Exploitive Use	Compulsive Achiever	Relaxed Achiever
Four Artist	Alienated & Tormented	Self-absorbed	Centered & Sensitive
Five Thinker	Strange Thoughts	Overly Analytical	Comfortable Expert
Six Loyal-Skeptic	Dependent Insecure	Traditionalist	Capable Loyal

Type	Dysfunctional	Normal	Healthy
Seven Optimist	Impulsive Escapist	Hyperactive Generalist	Adept (in several areas)
Eight Controller	Ruthless	Dominating	Powerful
Nine Peacemaker	Withdrawn and lethargic	Conforming of self	Supportive of self and others

DSM-III-R

BRIEF DESCRIPTIONS OF DIAGNOSTIC CATEGORIES

The mental disorder descriptions which follow are not precise *Diagnostic and Statistical Manual (DSM) of Mental Disorders* descriptions and do not relate exclusively to the Enneagram type in which they are listed. This material is intended to provide you with a brief understanding for how the particular disorder listed with each personality type is related more to the dysfunctional level in that particular personality type.

TYPE ONE-THE PERFECTIONIST

Obsessive-Compulsive Personality Disorder — Pervasive pattern of perfectionism and inflexibility, obsessed and driven to be perfect, excessively conscientious, moralistic, stingy and inflexible. **Obsessive-Compulsive Disorder** — Disturbed by intrusive obsessions such as "I could kill my child," or compulsions such as fear-driven compulsive hand washing.

TYPE TWO-THE PLEASER

Dependent Personality Disorder — Unable to independently make everyday decisions, easily hurt by criticism, and agrees with other people even when they know that the other person is wrong. **Conversion Disorder** — A physical dysfunction caused by a psychological conflict or need. For example, a person may develop blindness, seizures, or paralysis due to psychological conflict or need.

TYPE THREE-THE ACHIEVER

Narcissistic Personality Disorder — Grandiose, hypersensitive to evaluation by others, requires constant admiration, lacks empathy and is interpersonally exploitive.

TYPE FOUR-THE ARTIST

Borderline Personality Disorder — Despondency, anxiety, arrogance, dependency, defiance and unstable personal relationships.

TYPE FIVE-THE THINKER

Schizoid Personality Disorder — Pervasive pattern of indifference to social relationships and a restricted range of emotional experience and expression.

Schizotypal Personality Disorder — Peculiarities of ideation, appearance and defects in interpersonal relatedness. For example, becoming extremely anxious in social situations involving unfamiliar people and having bizarre thoughts.

TYPE SIX-THE LOYAL-SKEPTIC

Paranoid Personality Disorder — Pervasive and unwarranted tendency to interpret the actions of others as deliberately demeaning or threatening, holds grudges, easily slighted and reluctant to confide in others.

TYPE SEVEN-THE OPTIMIST

Hystronic Personality Disorder — Constantly seeks or demands approval or praise, shifting and shallow expression of emotions and flights into romantic fantasy.

TYPE EIGHT-THE CONTROLLER

Antisocial Personality Disorder — Impulsive, under-developed conscience, vindictive, performs antisocial acts, reckless, uses other people.

TYPE NINE-THE PEACEMAKER

Self-Defeating Personality — Life seems to require much effort and is generally unrewarding. For example, excessive and unrewarding self-sacrificing behavior is engaged in which is unsolicited by others. Attempts by others to treat them well are rejected.

Don't worry if you have identified with some of these behaviors at one time or another. However, if these behaviors are pervasive, not just isolated instances, then you might consider consulting a psychotherapist.

By now you probably have a much clearer understanding of your current level of psychological health and how much better your life can become if you decide to grow psychologically. In Appendix A, animal analogies are used to provide you with a way to gain additional insight into your level of health and what awaits you as you develop and grow. In the next chapter, obstacles which slow the process of transformation are discussed to help you recognize and overcome them more easily as you continue to grow and transform.

CHAPTER
14

OBSTACLES TO TRANSFORMATION

"The most difficult thing to do in life is to know yourself and to change yourself."

- Alfred Adler

A s you mature and become more clear, aware, and in touch with reality, you will move further along the path of transformation. Just as you may temporarily move into personality types which are different from your primary type, you may also temporarily be held back or retreat on your path of transformation. However, by increasing your self-awareness and the awareness of the obstacles to transformation which you will encounter, you become more free and your progress will ultimately move toward a more peaceful, effective state of being.

Understanding defense mechanisms as described by Sigmund Freud can provide you with insight into the ways you have created obstacles to reality and limited your life. Understanding these obstacles will help you overcome them and lay the foundation for you to utilize the techniques for transformation presented in Chapter 15.

211

Freud believed that when anxiety-provoking thoughts or feelings which you repressed in childhood begin to emerge, you use defense mechanisms to block or distort them. Blocking and distorting unconscious thoughts and feelings helps to keep you from feeling overwhelmed. By not admitting to your conscious mind that a situation or inner feeling is actually what it is, you try to avoid having to cope with or act on it. But, the reality which is attempting to express itself is often an aspect of yourself which needs to be faced to continue your growth.

Defense mechanisms operate quickly, automatically and without your conscious control. Their functioning is similar to your body's reflex response to a physical threat. If someone throws a rock at you, you automatically and without much conscious choice duck, turn, cover your face with your arms or take some other quick defensive maneuver to protect yourself.

You use defense mechanisms to cope with your everyday life. The healthier you are, the less you need to use them. If you rely on defense mechanisms too much, you may develop psychological problems such as overwhelming anxiety, or you may block the reality which is trying to express itself and instead try to maintain a distorted view of yourself and your environment, or you may use so much psychic energy defending yourself from reality that you don't have the energy required to cope with life. Your fixated personality is composed of your defenses against reality.

An appropriate use of defense mechanisms can help you balance the need to "not feel overwhelmed" with the need to "face reality." Overuse of defense mechanisms can lead to physical illness, emotional illness, and poor functioning in the world. In general, to transform yourself into higher level of health, you need to become aware of the ways you defend yourself against reality and to *gently* lower your defenses.

Defense Mechanisms

A discussion of the defense mechanisms (reaction formation, repression, identification, isolation, sublimation, projection, rationalization, denial, and narcotization) follows.

Most of the pairing of specific defense mechanisms with particular Enneagram types used in this book were developed by the psychiatrist Claudio Naranjo. Remember, **everyone** uses every defense mechanism to varying degrees all of the time.

Reaction Formation
(Inversion of Reality)

Reaction Formation occurs when you express behaviors or emotions which are the opposite of what you unconsciously experience. As with other defense mechanisms, you use them as a form of self-deception to protect yourself from thoughts and feelings which are unacceptable to you.

Type Ones, Perfectionists, are the most frequent users of reaction formation. For example, they often suppress their angry feelings toward someone, smile instead of frown and behave as if they simply want to help the other person change in order to improve the other person's life. Also, the public prudishness of Ones is often a sign of their defense against unconscious sexual feelings.

Repression
(Avoiding Reality)

Repression occurs when you keep anxiety-provoking thoughts or emotions at a distance in the unconscious. Repression is an aspect of all defense mechanisms. For example, in reaction formation, you first repress a thought or feeling and then behave the opposite way.

A child who feels very jealous of his brother may automatically and unconsciously prevent this intolerable thought from entering into his conscious mind. This repression of the

213

unacceptable thought does not mean that the hostility actually disappears. Repression helps the child's self-concept remain unblemished, at least temporarily and superficially.

Type Twos, Pleasers, use repression most frequently. Twos repress their own need for love and nurturance. They try to fulfill the needs of other people for love because they fear being abandoned. The energy required to repress their own needs and to fulfill other's needs is energy which they could utilize to love themselves and become more psychologically healthy.

IDENTIFICATION
(RELATING TO ANOTHER PERSON'S REALITY AS IF IT WERE YOUR OWN)

Identification happens when you adopt some other person's morality, values, successes and/or beliefs as your own. For example, if you identify with a television personality, when they feel good, you feel good. When they feel bad, you feel bad.

Type Threes, Achievers, use identification more than other types. Threes often identify with achieving people, whether in business, public office, entertainment or athletics as a way to bolster their own need to feel successful and to avoid feelings of failure. Sixes are doubtful of their own identity so they may "borrow" someone else's identity, or they may identify with some organization to feel more secure.

One of the major barriers to free essence is our identification with limited aspects of ourself or our environment. We feel that we *are* our job, our relationship, our body, or our personality. This limited, defensive and confused identification reduces our chance of seeing our whole, deeper, broader self and cuts us off from a larger range of freedom and joy in life.

SUBLIMATION
(RECHANNEL UNACCEPTABLE IMPULSES)

Sublimation is the re-direction of socially and personally unacceptable impulses into outlets which serve cultural or societal purposes.

Type Ones, Perfectionists, sublimate or redirect their anger into some *idealized* pursuit. Type Fours, Artists, use sublimation more often than other types. Their artistic expressions are often ways for them to rechannel the energy which is arising from repressed sexual feelings, anger and depression.

ISOLATION
(PARTITIONING REALITY)

Isolation is the way you separate anxiety-arousing emotions from thought. If you use it too extensively, you withdraw from emotions into thought, from your body into your head. Type Fives, Thinkers, use this defense mechanism more frequently than other types as a way to avoid feeling overwhelmed by emotions.

PROJECTION
(YOU SEE YOUR REALITY IN SOMEONE ELSE)

Another psychological defense mechanism is called projection. When you project, you attribute to another persons unconscious feelings or intentions which you don't want to face within yourself. Most of the thoughts which you have about other people are projections of your own disturbing internal thoughts. Many psychologists try to help their clients learn to "own" their problems and not to project them onto others. According to the psychiatrist Fritz Perls, the projector does unto others what they accuse the others of doing to them. Examples of projection follow:

Projection	Possible Unconscious Feelings
"Everyone lies."	I lie, or I am afraid to lie, or I want to lie.
"Why are you so angry at me?"	I am angry at you
"People are lazy."	I am lazy, or work hard to avoid being judged lazy by myself.

215

Another type of projection, which might also be called egocentrism, occurs when you try to give material or non-material things to other people that you, in reality, want for yourself. For example, someone who is being egocentric might give a camera attachment as a gift to his wife. But, guess who was the one who actually liked photography? The person giving the gift!

Type Nines, Peacemakers, try to avoid conflict. One of the non-material gifts which they may try to give to other people is a conflict-free life. Even though the other person's need for a conflict-free life is much less then that of the Type Nine, Nines try to help solve other's problems and go along with their wishes to make the other person's life easier.

Ones want to reform people along their own personal path of righteousness, a path which they know will "save" others. In reality, down deep, they fear that they themselves need to be saved.

Twos want others to feel loved and needed. The husband of a Type Two personality related, "We had been married for about one month when my wife said to me, "If you died, I would die." That's great news to another type Two, but for many people it's overwhelming to be needed that much.

Type Threes, Achievers, encourage others to achieve as they do. Type Fours, Artists, encourage others to experience artistic and original behavior. Type Fives, Thinkers, support others in academics. Type Sixes, Loyal-Skeptics, encourage people to be as loyal as they are. Type Sevens, Optimists, want everyone to be as lighthearted as they are. Type Eights, Controllers, believe everyone wants power and control as much as they do.

The paradox about projection and egocentric gift giving is that you don't really see the other person at all. You don't and can't see them as different from yourself, with different needs and desires. So what you give them or see them as needing is often *not* what they want or need, but what you really want for yourself.

What a world. You give gifts to others which you really want or need, while at the same time you often remain unaware of your own wants and needs.

All personality types use projection as a defense mechanism to some extent. Sixes with their suspiciousness about the intentions of others, are the most frequent users of projection. Sixes don't trust their inner nature. They project this distrust onto their environment and become suspicious about other people.

RATIONALIZATION
(REDEFINE REALITY)

Rationalization is the process of developing "believable" excuses and using distorted logic to make thoughts and behaviors which we believe unconsciously are unacceptable to our conscious mind. Type Sevens, Optimists, use rationalization more than other types to justify their optimistic, light-hearted behavior as well as their outbursts of anger.

DENIAL
(REFUSAL TO FACE REALITY)

Denial is an attempt to distort reality concerning some thought which is unacceptable to your self-concept. Alcoholics often use denial. After they finish drinking a case of beer, they attempt to convince themselves and others that they've just had a few cans.

Type Eights, Controllers, are the most frequent users of denial. To avoid facing their inner feelings of vulnerability, they deny their inner feelings of weakness.

NARCOTIZATION
(NUMBING REALITY)

Narcotization lowers your general awareness of anxiety and other feelings such as anger. Type Nines, Peacemakers, use narcotization to avoid feelings which arise when they face conflict and begin to feel anger. For example, a Nine may use food, sleep and/or television to lower their awareness of anger. However, anger can't be isolated from power and other "juicy emotions," so Nines inadvertently shut down essential energies such as those of power and sex.

DEFENSE MECHANISM SUMMARY

You use defense mechanisms to block, soften or distort reality so that you won't be overwhelmed. Every personality type uses all of the defense mechanisms discussed to protect their fixated personality shell. However, each Enneagram personality type and each individual person relies more heavily on one or more defense mechanisms.

The optimum approach is to use defense mechanisms enough to feel comfortable, but not so much that we become drained of energy by repressing our feelings and becoming too-out-of-touch with reality.

Defense mechanisms are one example of the many obstacles to transformation. Other obstacles include unreasonable expectations of yourself and others, enticingly pleasurable experiences, false leaders, transference, pride, competition, over-dependence, under-dependence, overbearing superego, anger, fear and impatience.

The tools for self-transformation introduced in the next chapter can help you overcome all of these obstacles. As was mentioned in the introduction to Part Three, the written discussion about these tools is brief. In fact, they may seem simple. And in concept they are. However, these tools are extremely powerful and can soften and dissolve defense mechanisms and other obstacles to transformation. They are transformative when you practice them regularly. In Chapter 15 you are encouraged to delve into your inner self with the aid of some brief exercises to experience tools which lead to transformation. Transformation is experimental or existential rather than intellectual. The purpose of all of these tools for transformation is to help you delve deeply into yourself.

DELVING INWARD

"There has never been a religion founded, never a good book written, never a good picture painted, never a good poem composed, never a good intention developed, except by going inside to some extent, and there concentrating on the task at hand."

- Julian Johnson

M any different methods of observing yourself can help you delve into the depths of your being and help release more of your essence. The methods introduced in this chapter include seeking the truth, understanding emotions, placement of attention, meditation, and developing presence. All "delving inward" methods focus on what is happening to you now in the present moment.

As you master some of these methods and delve deeper and deeper into yourself, you become more relaxed and yet alert. Delving deeper helps you loosen the constraints of your fixated personality shell and develop a deeper understanding of yourself and others. It helps you become more present, releases energy which has been trapped in body constrictions due to unresolved childhood conflicts and become more spacious, loving and energetic. All of these benefits of delving inward lead you to greater contact with and release of your essence.

DELVING INWARD WITH TRUTH

"The true lover of knowledge must, from childhood up, be most of all a striver after truth in every form."

- Plato

Seeking the truth leads to love and transformation. It helps you "delve" inward to the center of your being. If your intentions are based on a sincere effort to seek the true fundamental reality about yourself and life, you will gain greater inner clarity and proceed further on the path of transformation.

If you seek anything other than the truth as a basis for personal growth, you will be laboring in vain. For example, if your primary purpose in pursuing personal growth is to change yourself instead of simply seeking the truth about yourself, you are in effect rejecting yourself as you are now. You don't think that you are okay as you are now. Putting pressure on yourself to change and grow based on rejecting yourself as you are now or viewing yourself as not being okay is the most frequently used approach to self-improvement. However, it usually doesn't produce substantial or lasting results. The following is an attempt to clarify this often misunderstood concept.

People grow and expand most readily when they are supported, loved and accepted. They contract and become less happy when they are judged and criticized. They don't usually want to be around people who judge and criticize them, even if it is criticism which is intended to be "for their own good."

You respond to your thoughts and feelings about yourself in the same way that you respond to other people's thoughts and feelings about you. You feel good, grow and expand when you love and accept yourself. When you judge or criticize yourself you reject yourself, leading to lower self-esteem.

The way we normally try to change others is to make suggestions for their improvement (criticize). In effect, we are telling them that their are aspects of themselves which they should reject. They aren't okay as they are now. It seems logical and it is the most often used approach to change other people.

But it doesn't work the way we hope it will! Especially if we are trying to achieve meaningful lasting growth which requires the release of your or someone else's essence.

For example, you may convince your spouse to stay home more by criticizing, nagging and threatening - in effect, you are telling your spouse that he or she isn't okay. He or she isn't a good spouse because they don't stay home more. Your efforts may even appear to work. However, it definitely *will* lower their self-esteem. And you *will* become a negative, painful stimulus in their environment. On the surface, or deep down and unconsciously, they will want to be around you less. Your efforts to change them backfires. They may or may not stay home more. But, either way, they *will* at some level be angry or resentful toward you.

The traditional answer of behavioral psychology to the problem in the above example and similar problems is to encourage the person who wants to change the behavior of their spouse to use positive reinforcement. Instead of criticizing their spouse, reward them with praise, presents or compliments when they do what you want them to do (in this case stay home more) and ignore them when they don't.

Positive reinforcement is a wonderful improvement over criticism as a way to produce change. Experiments by behavioral psychologists prove that positive reinforcement works well to modify behavior. So it is very likely that the person could condition (change) their spouse to stay home more by using positive reinforcement. Their spouse's self-esteem would improve because they were being praised instead of criticized, and their spouse would want to be around their partner more. They would stay home more, enjoy home life more, like the person more and like themself more. However, even though the person is using a positive approach to change their spouse, the person is actually controlling their spouse and changing their spouse's behavior to suit their own needs. The person is channeling and restricting the free and natural growth of their spouse. In the most negative sense, they are manipulating their partner.

Self-criticism as a way to produce change and personal

growth usually lowers self-esteem and thereby undermines future interest in change and growth. Positive reinforcement is a "nicer" method than criticism to try to produce change and personal growth. However, it still has drawbacks. For example, it restricts free and natural growth. Seeking the truth goes beyond criticism and positive reinforcement and the results are more growth-producing. Seeking the truth doesn't involve criticism nor the attempt to control anyone's behavior. It encourages delving into and exploring the problem or issue to discover the truth about it.

In the case of the person who wanted their spouse to stay home more, this approach encourages both people to seek the truth about the problem with no overt or hidden agenda to criticize or change anyone. The person may discover that their spouse is angry, overwhelmed or that they thought their partner didn't really want them around. The goal is to discover the truth about the issues involved, not change the situation according to one spouse's desires.

Seeking the truth will lead to a solution or resolution of the problem. However, the solution may not be the solution which the person had hoped for. But seeking the truth will produce more clarity and greater understanding about the problem and the relationship. And it will lead to the most appropriate solution. This approach is the basis for intimacy and love. No one was criticized, and no one was controlled. The relationship will become more rewarding. And each person will grow and expand.

When you "delve" into your innermost being, now, in this moment, to gain insights for self-transformation, the issues which you encounter are often much more sensitive than the problem of wanting your spouse to stay home more. You may encounter issues such as fear of failure, anger about your childhood, hate or deep feelings of inadequacy. So, self-rejection, control and criticism need to be avoided even more when working with these more delicate and deep psychological issues encountered along the path of transformation.

Delving inward with self-positive reinforcement or praising

yourself as a way to improve yourself is a subtle way to control and direct your personal development. In effect, it becomes a restriction to your personal freedom and your ability to expand and unfold in the most natural and effective way.

So don't try to change yourself using criticism or positive reinforcement. Slow down, shift your attention inward and seek the truth about who you are, about what is happening now in your life. The light of truth dissolves problems, leaves heightened awareness and clearer understanding. Your essence will sense the embrace of your love for truth and self-acceptance, and it will expand, grow and you will become more healthy and free.

The awareness exercise which follows was designed to help you get a *glimpse* using truth to explore an issue which relates to your life. To benefit the most from "delving" into yourself, discovering the truth about yourself, you need to explore something which you are experiencing now, at this moment. Exploring what happened at any other time is intellectual speculation, rather than a direct experience of reality. Exploring the truth about any aspect of you or your life now, at this very moment, is the most useful approach to transformation.

AWARENESS EXERCISE

Delve into the truth about some current, important issue in life by filling in the blank in the sentence "What is the truth about my _____?" with a current personal issue such as fear of being alone, getting married or becoming a failure.

Ask yourself this question ten times. Each time write down the **first** thought, feeling or emotion which you experience. Write down the **first** thing which comes to your mind, even if it doesn't seem important or make sense. The more spontaneous the answer, the greater the truth.

1.

2.

3.

4.

5.

6.

7.

8.

9.

10.

What new insights into your personal issue did you obtain by doing this exercise?

DELVING INWARD WITH EMOTIONS

Emotions are your engine, your energy of motion at the level of the nervous system. When your emotions are repressed and aren't completely discharged after being aroused, your emotions and the thoughts which are part of your emotions produce psychological boundaries. Boundaries are the limits you place on your emotional availability to protect yourself from being overwhelmed. Boundaries define your capacity to make contact with other people and the world. They form the basis for your fixated personality. When emotions discharge, they ultimately soften boundaries, increase love, and enhance relaxation.

Beneath the surface of your personality, fixations, boundaries and desires, lies something much larger, more valuable and beautiful. It's as if you've been living in the attic of your personal mansion since birth. However, you haven't realized that there are many other rooms still left to be explored. You are not whole and only live in a very small part of yourself.

The rooms are locked by your anxiety based defense mechanisms. Some of the rooms are locked tightly while other rooms seem too dark and too scary to even think of opening. When you initially open the doors and turn on the lights, you might experience emotional pain and confusion. However, if you can be brave and experience your emotions as they arise, with the aid of understanding they will discharge, you will feel more free, you will begin to see more clearly through your fixated personality shell and you will release more of your essence. You will love and become more intimate with your mansion. If you continue your growth and transformation long enough, the walls of your mansion will dissolve completely, and you will be free.

George Gurdjieff called facing inner fears and unpleasant emotions "conscious suffering." Others call it "creative suffering" because it leads to growth and aliveness in your life. This "creative suffering" contrasts with neurotic suffering which is due to your attempts to fulfill the desires of your fixated personality shell. For example, if you are a Type Seven personality and "suffer" because your plans for fun are interfered with, this suffering will be repeated over and over again every time your plans are interfered with. However, if you have suffered (felt angry, sad or anxious) while gaining insights into yourself and discover why you need to continuously plan to avoid psychological pain, the overall amount of suffering and pain in your life will lessen.

The pain of "creative suffering" is like the pain a mother experiences when giving birth to a child. It comes as you understand yourself more and your essence emerges, is "birthed" into the world. You are giving "birth" to creative, new and clearer insights and understandings about yourself which free you from repeating your pursuit of desires which are repetitive and based on fear. So, be brave, open the doors of your mansion, turn on the lights and face your fears. Let more of your essence be released, expand and grow.

You don't have to be brave like John Wayne and try to encounter your fears alone. *Everyone* needs help and support to make significant progress. Your support can be a trusted friend, spouse, psychotherapist, minister or support group. As you grow and develop, you may move from the person you initially sought for support to someone more advanced. Don't go frantically searching for a more advanced teacher because, as the ancients knew, "When the student is ready, the teacher will appear."

EMOTIONS FROM THE PERSPECTIVE OF THE ENNEAGRAM

The intensity and type of emotions which you experience are a prime indicator of your personality type. Some people, such as Type Fours, are generally overwhelmed by too many intense emotions. Others, like Type Fives, are "cut off" from their emotions.

Most psychologists believe that emotions involve distinct changes in the body and the mind. Thoughts and body sensations both occur at about the same time. There is substantial disagreement about whether it is the body or the mind which reacts to the emotion-arousing stimulus first.

Emotions as they relate to the Enneagram personality types will be briefly discussed next. Anger, anxiety and depression are emphasized because they are the primary emotional issues of people in the gut, head and heart centers.

ANGER

Your **anger** is a strong feeling of displeasure and antagonism based on your frustration that the world is not the way you think that it should be. You feel that you have been wronged or you are not getting your way. Anger is usually felt energetically in the belly or gut. **Everyone**, on a daily basis, either consciously or unconsciously, experiences anger.

As was explored in Chapter Eight, anger is the primary emotional issue which underlies the compelling drive and perception of the Gut Center personalities (Types Eight, Nine and One). The Type Eights, Controllers, externalize anger and express it most openly and directly. Nines, Peacemakers, deaden anger and become passive-aggressive. Ones, Perfectionists, internalize anger in the form of an "inner critic" and make any external expression of anger legitimate by being "right."

ANXIETY

Anxiety is a fearful feeling based on uncertainty perceived to be in the environment. It is based on a lack of trust that the world is fair and predictable. It usually produces worry and an avoidance response. However, it can also lead to the opposite - an attack. For example, you shouldn't corner a frightened animal, even if it is a small animal such as a cat. Because you are bigger, it will usually hide or retreat. However, if it is trapped and very anxious, it may launch an unpredictable and ferocious attack.

We *all* experience anxiety in some form every day, either consciously or unconsciously. Yes, even the powerful Type Eights! Eights' anxiety relates to fear of being vulnerable and unjustly controlled, so they control their environment to prevent

227

it from unjustly controlling them.

Anxiety is most often associated with the thinking types: Five, Six and Seven. Fives think to avoid feelings of anxiety which emerges when they begin to feel their emotions. Sixes, Loyal-Skeptics, avoid and try to reduce their anxious feelings by projecting their fear into their environment. Because of their projected fear, they view other people and their environment as untrustworthy. Sevens, Optimists, avoid painful emotions and anxiety by dwelling on pleasant plans for the future the happy side of life and keeping busy.

Sixes exhibit anxiety most visibly. In fact, you often can see anxiety in their eyes, a look similar to that of a scared rabbit. On the other hand, the behavior of many Sixes is anything but fearful. They take risks climbing mountains, rescuing victims and fighting with other people. In psychological terminology, these brave Sixes are called counter-phobic. Their brave behavior is the opposite of how they actually feel inside.

DEPRESSION

Depression includes feelings of sadness and dejection. It is often accompanied by loss of energy, crying, feelings of hopelessness and worthlessness. As with all emotions, we *all* experience depression at some level of severity daily. In fact, depression has been called the "common cold" of the emotional world. One of the primary causes of depression is loss. For example, loss of a loved one, income or hope can trigger depression. Another major cause is frustration. Depression is often experienced in the body as a heavy sensation in the chest.

Types Two, Three and Four personalities need to feel valued in the eyes of other people. When they lose what they believe others value in them, they tend to feel depressed. When a Type Two, Pleaser, feels their giving isn't valued, or when a Type Three, Achiever, feels their success isn't enough, or when a Type Four, Artist, doesn't feel they are unique or special enough, these types are prone to depression. Fours generally experience feelings of depression and mood swings. On the downside of their mood swing, depression tends to be intense.

DELVING INTO EMOTIONS

According to Carl Jung, "Emotion is the chief source of all becoming conscious. There can be no transforming of darkness into light and of apathy into movement without emotions." Delving into emotions is a major door into your inner self and a vital aid in the transformation process. A.H. Almaas describes emotions as a guide to where "essence has been lost."

All emotions are interrelated and layered in depth inside of you, so any of them can be used as a place to delve deeper into yourself. For example, as you delve deeper into yourself, anger may shift into sadness and fear may shift into anger. This discussion is intended to provide you with a glimpse into the interrelatedness of emotions and the value of being aware of and working through your emotions to your essence which underlies them.

The interrelationship of emotions is more easily revealed in a supportive, therapeutic setting. For example, if someone's initial emotion is anger and they express it in a therapeutic setting for an appropriate amount of time (delves deep enough) they usually begin to cry and to express the underlying hurt feelings which they were afraid to make contact with or to express initially. If the person continues their emotional release (delves further), they usually complete the process by feeling content and experiencing a sense of well-being. They develop a clearer awareness of themselves. So, under the anger was fear, and under the fear was sadness, and under the sadness was hurt, and under the hurt was contentment.

The exact order is not always the same. You may be sad and crying. As you delve inside to become aware of what triggered your sadness, you may become angry or feel guilty. However, fear – based on lack of basic trust – is always present at a deep level. It is the ultimate barrier between the other emotions and awareness, resolution and contentment. Isn't it reassuring to know that feelings of love and contentment generally arise when emotions are delved into sufficiently?

This is what psychotherapists call "working through" emotions to obtain insight and resolution. The alternative is to "stuff" emotions. The price for stuffing emotions is lack of awareness, unnecessary draining of psychological energy to avoid the issue, unnecessary draining of physical energy due to tight muscles in the body, inner turmoil, conflicts, lack of contentment and sometimes physical illness.

At a deeper, transformational level, emotional work can become a window or opening to your essence. For example, if you become angry and frustrated because someone else got a job which you wanted, you might discover that underneath the anger is sadness and underneath the sadness is your deep fear that you aren't strong enough, and of sufficient value to be worthy of the job you were seeking.

Traditional therapy would stop at this point. In more transformationally oriented therapy, you would be encouraged to delve deeper into feelings to feel lack of strength and lack of worth and to ultimately make contact with your essence. If you stay with your uncomfortable feelings long enough, you may experience a void, hole or emptiness. If you stay with the void long enough, it will transform mere deficient emptiness to inner spaciousness and in that opening space an aspect of your essence can emerge, such as essential strength, and you will become inwardly stronger and more self-confident.

Therefore, if you delve deep enough into your anger, you gain psychological understanding, and became more relaxed and content because of the discharge of your emotions. After you experience your feelings of incompetence and weakness and the underlying experience of emptiness, you regain some of the essential strength you had lost touch with early in childhood.

DELVING INWARD USING MEDITATION

Meditation is another method to delve inward. It involves observing an inner processes such as physical body sensations, breathing, thoughts or emotions.

When you practice meditation, regardless of which inner process you observe, you will begin to discover where you are most tense and relaxed in your body. You will become more aware of your patterns of thinking and how they relate to body tension and what triggers your emotions. If you are patient and practice long enough and consistently, you may notice that your mental health increases, your relationships improve, your concentration becomes better, you feel less anxious and more alert and you make contact with your essence with less effort.

Like developing any other skill or capacity, it is best to learn meditation with an experienced teacher. But, if you want to practice on your own, use the following instructions to assist you in your endeavor.

1. Practice when you first awaken in the morning, when your mind and environment are generally quiet.

2. Locate a comfortable quiet space in which to practice.

3. If you are sitting in a chair, sit with your back upright and feet flat on the floor.

4. If you are sitting on the floor, cross your legs and hold your back in an upright position.

5. Rest your hands on your legs, palms up.

6. Gently close your eyes.

7. Now is the time to observe an inner process. Observing the rise and fall of your belly as you breath is a good practice to begin with.

8. Observe the rise and fall of your belly for at least five minutes.

The benefits of meditation increases as the unbroken time of involvement increases and when you practice daily instead of occasionally. Practicing for a minimum of twenty minutes per session and on a daily basis for a month is usually needed to feel the power of meditation.

In the awareness exercises that follow, the first meditation practice is counting from one to ten as you exhale. This meditation practice, like the practice of watching the rise and fall of your belly, is a good self-observation practice for the beginner. The numbers from one to ten are to be counted with each exhale of your breath. If you become distracted, which is very likely, and lose track of your count before reaching the number ten, begin counting all over again with the number one. If you reach the number ten or accidently count higher than the number ten, begin counting all over again starting with the number one. Be gentle with yourself. Don't judge yourself for miscounting, over counting or losing count - everyone does. You will accomplish the task of meditation when you are sincere in your efforts, not by striving for perfection.

In subsequent parts of this awareness exercise you will observe your thoughts, body and emotions. The first aspect of yourself which you will practice observing is your thoughts, because your mind is very active, and thoughts are usually the easiest aspect of yourself to observe. Next, you will observe your body sensations. As you go beyond noticing the states of tightness and relaxation in your body, your awareness will be drawn to noticing subtle body energies. Finally, you will concentrate on the combination of thoughts and body feelings, called emotions, a much more difficult inner dimension to observe.

The process you will use for meditation of your thoughts,

body sensations and emotions will be similar to that used by Freud when he asked patients to verbally free associate by expressing anything and everything that came into their minds. When you meditate on your thoughts in the awareness exercise which follows, you will simply observe your thoughts. You won't express them verbally. After each thought, body sensation or emotion, you need to say to yourself, "It's okay to let go." This statement encourages your mind to relax and let the next thought, body sensation or emotion emerge into your awareness.

AWARENESS EXERCISE
MEDITATION

Describe your thinking and your breathing pattern as they were before, during, and immediately after the five-minute **counting concentration** exercise. Count from one to ten. Use each exhalation for one count. If you count beyond ten or forget your count, start over again at one.

Describe your thoughts and your breathing pattern as they were before, during, and immediately after the five-minute **thought** self-observation exercise. Notice thoughts as they arise. And, as you exhale, say to yourself: "It's okay to let go." Repeat the process.

AWARENESS EXERCISE
MEDITATION

Describe your thoughts and your breathing pattern as they were before, during, and immediately after the five-minute **body** self-observation exercise. Notice each body sensation, comfortable or uncomfortable, as it arises in your body. And, as you exhale, say to yourself: "It's okay to let go."

Describe your thoughts and your breathing pattern as they were before, during, and immediately after the five-minute **emotion** self- observation exercise. Notice the emotions in your body-mind. And, as you exhale, say to yourself: "It's okay to let go."

DELVING INWARD USING PLACEMENT OF ATTENTION

Attention is the focusing of awareness or consciousness. Most of the time your attention shifts to a particular dimension of your mind, body or emotions without your conscious control. You may be attending to the future, the past or emotions without a conscious choice or awareness. In effect, you don't know where you are (where your attention is placed), and you aren't in control of your attention.

Where are you right now? Your attention was probably on this book. Or, maybe it was placed on some worries about the future and, even though you continue to read the book, you (your attention) is not fully here. Or, maybe you were recalling an exciting moment in the past. Being aware of where you "are" and where your attention tends to shift to increases self-understanding and the chance that you can be where you really want to be. For example, the Type Nines' attention easily drifts into fantasy, making it difficult to concentrate. As they become more aware of these frequent shifts of attention to fantasy, they automatically become more capable of staying present in the moment and capable of concentrating on what they choose to concentrate on.

The attention awareness exercise which follows is based on one which the Enneagram teacher Helen Palmer uses to help her students become more aware of the places where they most often place their attention: in the environment, inside themselves, in the future, in the past, in images or fantasy, in emotions and in physical senses. The last placement of attention introduced is similar to an aspect of the "work" used at the Ridhwan school of A.H. Almaas as a way to help people become more fully aware in the present moment. It is the placement of your attention in your arms and legs while going about your everyday life.

Attention Placement Exercise

To increase your awareness about your placement of attention, have someone read you the following instructions while your eyes are closed.

1. Shift your attention out to about an arm's length in front of you (imagine yourself being at the end of your arm).

2. Shift your attention inward (actually direct your eyes inward, toward the inside of your belly).

3. Shift your attention to a memory. Become aware of the details in your memory including color, sound, and other people.

4. Shift your attention to a future plan.

5. Shift to a fantasy image. Try a beach or mountain scene.

6. Notice your emotional state while your attention is at the beach or mountain.

7. Notice the sensations of sunshine or a breeze on your face.

Most people recall that as they shifted from one placement of attention to another, the existing placement of attention was dissolved. Then, their attention became fixated on, and they identified with, the new placement of attention. Usually, we become so identified with one placement of attention that we become unaware of other possible placement of attention. For example, we become so aware of an emotion that we forget that we have a mind to think with and may behave inappropriately based on the emotion.

Try this exercise again, beginning with step one. Become more aware of how your shifts of attention occur. Notice how you often become completely immersed in, and identified with, each placement.

Discuss what you experienced while completing this exercise.

Check the location where you place your awareness most of the time.

(   ) Outside of yourself,
(   ) Inward,
(   ) Past memory,
(   ) Future plan,
(   ) Emotions,
(   ) Physical senses,
(   ) Fantasy.

PRESENCE

PLACEMENT OF ATTENTION TO YOUR ARMS AND LEGS

The psychiatrist Fritz Perls emphasized the value of living "here and now," living each moment to its fullest. After all, the present moment is all that you have. When you are in your mind excessively planning the future or dwelling on the past, you are rejecting the fullest possibility for aliveness which you have right now. You are rejecting your life as it is now.

One of the uses of the attention practice which follows is to help keep you present in the here and now, and to alert you to when you aren't present, because generally when you aren't present you won't be feeling your arms and legs. Even though it may not seem like it could help your process of transformation very much, it will when you practice it regularly. It is an extremely powerful tool for developing presence, a clearer understanding of yourself and a sharper awareness of your environment.

One of the best things about this practice is that, unlike other self-observation practices which you may practice only occasionally or for a fixed period of time, this practice can become part of your everyday life as your commitment to inner work grows. You can use it through out the day and night, alone or with someone else, at work or at play.

AWARENESS EXERCISE
FEELING YOUR ARMS AND LEGS

One morning, before you start your day, sit down and close your eyes. Then place your attention on the bottom of your right foot. When your attention is there try to feel some physical sensation such as coolness, warmth or a tingling. Then spread this inner awareness to your entire right foot, slowly spread it up your right leg to your knee and then spread it up to your hip.

Next, shift your attention to your right upper arm. Wait until you can feel a physical sensation in your upper arm. Spread the sensations down your right arm into your hand and into each finger. Do the same procedure with the left arm. Shift your attention to your left hip. Let the awareness spread down your left leg and into your left foot. Now expand your awareness to feel both arms and both legs at the same time.

Keep feeling your arms and legs while you slowly open your eyes. If you are unable to feel them, close your eyes again and try to regain the sensations in your arms and legs. Open your eyes again and try to maintain your awareness of the feelings in your arms and legs.

In the blank space provided below describe what you experienced as you did this awareness exercise.

On the day you experienced the arms and legs exercise, remind yourself to notice your arms and legs every hour. See if you can sense them while you are walking, riding in a car or sitting at work. Try to feel them while you are talking or listening to someone else.

Were you able during the day to continuously sense your arms and legs? When was it easy and when was it difficult to sense them?

In what situations were you more present (more aware of your arms and legs)?

Part Three of this book focused on transformation, the process of moving inward and identifying more with your essence than your fixated personality shell. The insights and exercises presented were designed to provide you with a brief introduction to the basic tools for transformation. Transformation is a life long adventure which explores the mysteries of life and moves you closer and closer to living a life of celebration. To fully benefit from these tools you need to practice frequently and ultimately make them a part of your life. For example, practicing feeling your arms and legs to become more present can be viewed as similar to muscle building exercises. When building bigger muscles, the more you exercise the larger your muscles become. Likewise, when building presence, the more you practice feeling your arms and legs, the stronger and more lasting your presence becomes.

The final chapter summarizes the most important themes in this book and encourages you to continue your self-growth and inner-transformation.

16

THE CELEBRATION OF LIFE

*"What lies behind us and what lies before us are small
compared to what lies within us."*
- Ralph Waldo Emerson

Ralph Waldo Emerson expresses the value of shifting our attention inward in the present moment. Delving inward to shed the light of truth on our moment-to-moment experience will free us from the restrictive aspects of our personality and allow us to more freely express our true self, our essence. Life becomes a **"stepping out from within."**

Remember, you are not attempting to get rid of your personality. Your goal is to loosen the constrictions of your fixated personality, while keeping its healthy parts, as you open to your essence. You want to integrate the healthy aspects of all nine personality types on the Enneagram to realize your personal potential. The ideal is to become a balanced, integrated and fulfilled expression of who you really are. When you do, your life will become a moment-to-moment celebration.

Guided by the wisdom of the ancient Enneagram map and modern psychodynamic psychology contained in this book, your journey will ultimately lead you to a maturity, a humanity, a wisdom which will guide you to a celebration of life to its fullest.

As you progress on this journey, you will act on the world more according to your inner nature rather than reacting defensively to the demands of the world. You will develop inner peace, confidence and the strength needed to continue to free your essence and transcend your personality. You will move to the deepest truths and understandings about yourself, truths which will free you from your childhood-based, fixated personality. You will perceive, accept and rejoice in reality as you experience it moment-to-moment.

The flow of this book is patterned after the journey of growth and transformation and is similar to the natural flow of life for those who awaken to their dilemma and begin the journey home to their true nature. In the beginning of the journey, you need and seek simple and readily understandable concepts such as offered in Part One, which you can count on to help you grow.

In the middle of the path you need and are attracted to ideas and concepts which are broader, deeper, appeal more to your emotions and allow more for your individuality such as those offered in Part Two.

Toward the end of the journey, in Part Three, you probe deeper into life and move inward along a footpath which you travel alone. You find that looking inward is the most direct path to your essence, the ground of your being, the place where lasting joy, happiness, love and peace radiate. It is a place which can only be pointed to, a place which only can be fully understood by direct experience.

REFLECTIONS ON PART I – INITIAL SELF-UNDERSTANDING

The initial introduction to the Enneagram, Personality Development and Essence, is usually greeted with a mixture of excitement and fear. You begin by making contact with the idea that you are stuck, like the scorpion, with fixated behaviors. This truth is exciting and disheartening.

It is exciting to begin to see how stuck you are in your personality type, because love and compassion for yourself and others begin to emerge as you feel the reduction in your guilt about who you are and what you do. You reduce your tendency to blame others for who they are and what they do. You begin to let go of outdated reactions to your environment. And you begin to see how much energy you waste by trying to change others to make them have a personality and values like yours. As this happens, you have more energy, life becomes easier and love flows more effortlessly.

On the other hand, you may become disheartened. You may feel that you are stuck in your personality as a Controller, Perfectionist, Achiever, or whatever your personality type is, for life. You may feel frustrated and hopeless.

But, when you realize that your essence is buried inside your fixated personality shell and that as you move along your path it is released, you become inspired to move forward in the transformational process. You are likely to be eager to experience the joy, love and peace that are aspects of your essence. Essence remains a concept at this stage of your journey, rather than something which you can access and release easily.

For people at this stage, personal growth is usually a struggle, but they persist. They begin to realize that following their compelling desire is a never ending circle of hope, with just brief experiences of well-being and frequent disappointment. In reality, they are going nowhere. Only hope for a better life keeps them going.

REFLECTIONS ON PART TWO – DEEPENING, INTEGRATING, AND LOVING

Part Two goes into more detail on the Enneagram and encourages you to discover how your personality type penetrates everything you do, from the way you think, feel and act, to a deeper understanding of your way of relating to others. It provides greater clarity about the specific ways you use to cope as a child, whether it was trying to take charge, accommodate or become self-sufficient.

It helps you to understand that the only way to attain significant and lasting improvements in your relationships, to find the right person and live a deeply loving life, arises from the increased personal health which comes from knowing and loving yourself more.

You discover that knowing and loving yourself more leads to more fulfilling relationships. The more you love yourself, the more likely you are to have a relationship based on Being Love (fulfilling love) instead of Deficiency Love (painful co-dependency love). Your relationships become more mutually fulfilling.

The rewards for gaining greater self-knowledge become more obvious as you read this part of the book. The self-acceptance and understanding lead to more comfortable and rewarding relationships and a happier, more rewarding life. As a result, growth during this stage takes place with greater confidence and commitment. You develop a thirst for greater awareness and depth in life.

REFLECTIONS ON PART THREE – LOOKING INWARD

In Part Three, the necessity of shifting your attention inward to travel the road of transformation is stressed. The wide highway of the Enneagram narrows to a personal footpath which only you can travel. Methods such as meditation and being present are introduced to help you "delve" inward. Your interest is shifted from self-improvement and gaining understanding of your personality type, which is more the focus of psychology, to discovering the truth about yourself, the human condition and transformation, which are more the focus of spirituality.

You become aware that as you delve inward, when you are guided by a love of truth, your progress accelerates. You become more and more aware of how unaware and restricted you have been in your personality. You feel like you have been lost and are now coming home. You can feel yourself blossoming. Life becomes more like a dance and celebration of love than an effort to be liked and happy. Growth comes from surrendering to the truth and an expansion of love. What you thought was your personal potential becomes a base for moving to even greater and greater expansion and transformation. You free yourself from your efforts to force change in yourself and others. Transformation is felt as an adventure filled with excitement and danger as you move inward to the essence of your being. Everything in existence becomes beautiful in its own way. You love yourself and life more and more and more.

The further you travel along the road of transformation, the more important guidance and support become. For an initial understanding, a book will do well to clarify and sharpen your self-understanding. To attain a deep understanding of yourself, workshops and/or the help of a psychotherapist is usually necessary. To fully engage in the transformation process by shifting from over-identification with your personality to identifying more with your essence typically requires the assistance of a teacher experienced in guiding people engaged in the transformation process.

Regardless of how you decide to pursue the path, on your own or with the aid of a therapist or teacher, your experience of love will grow as your awareness deepens. There are no words that can adequately describe the sweet love which comes from deep inner awareness. Aspects of essence such as compassion, strength and joy flourish in the embrace of love.

The more aware you become as you travel closer to home,

the easier and more quickly you will develop new awareness. It becomes easier and easier to see the world with sharp, accurate perception. Essence permeates more and more throughout your being. There is no end to the mystery which is life nor to the rewards which come from exploring the mystery with a heart which longs for truth.

APPENDIX A
ANIMAL ANALOGIES
FOR LEVELS OF
PSYCHOLOGICAL HEALTH

The characteristics of animals, birds and insects are introduced as analogies for personality styles. They are an enjoyable way to help you develop a better understanding of the levels of psychological health (the psychotic, dysfunctional, normal, healthy and free levels) for all nine Enneagram personality types.

The experience of the psychotic and free levels are similar for all Enneagram types. So, only one analogy is used to describe the free and psychotic levels for all nine Enneagram types.

At the **psychotic level**, people are helplessly trapped in the illusion of their personality out of fear. They are lost in a non-reality which often includes delusions and hallucinations. They are caught like a helpless *insect in a black widow's web.*

At the **free level**, people fearlessly disidentify with their personality. They connect with their essence and have a clear and direct perception of truth and reality. They love all of life and are as free as a *bird*, a bird which has left the imprisonment of its cage where its wings were useless, song was empty, energy was shutdown, and it parroted what it was taught to survive and gain attention.

Analogies for the dysfunctional, normal and healthy levels of health for each Enneagram type follow. Certain characteristics of these analogies are used to portray each level of health. The characteristics of each analogy are meant to be symbolic rather than precise and accurate representations of particular personalities.

TYPE ONE - THE PERFECTIONIST

DYSFUNCTIONAL	NORMAL	HEALTHY
Chicken	Domesticated Horse	Beaver

The dysfunctional chicken is scattered, jumpy and worried about covering every square inch of ground in its environment. It is constantly running around to keep things under control. It is exhausted and confused. It pecks at (judges) everything. The domesticated horse is serious, it works hard and does what it is expected to do. It will even try to reform untamed horses to help them set high standards and to do good work. The healthy beaver works conscientiously and easily at growing and building. It conserves its strength, can take breaks, concentrates on the most meaningful task and doesn't set unreasonably high goals. It is tolerant of the behavior of other beavers

TYPE 2 - THE PLEASER

DYSFUNCTIONAL	NORMAL	HEALTHY
Oyster	Lhasa Apso	Mother Kangaroo

The dysfunctional oyster entices people into loving relationships with their rare pearl of a heart. Then they painfully clamp on and won't let go. They feel like a victim because they feel that sharing their pearl is worth far more than what anyone can share in return. The normal Lhasa Apso dog is friendly, overly loving and always wants to be with someone. It becomes fearful, unmotivated and sad when no one special is around. The healthy mother kangaroo is nurturing, but not possessive. It is loving and enjoys its child, yet it feels its own sense of well-being even when there is no child in its pouch. It encourages its child (mate or friend) to hop around on its own two feet.

TYPE 3 - THE ACHIEVER

DYSFUNCTIONAL	NORMAL	HEALTHY
Chameleon	Race Horse	Hawk

The dysfunctional chameleon *does not* change the color of its personality to disappear and blend in. It wants to fake a personality that will help it stand out and be valued and admired in every environment which it encounters. It is deceptive and exploitative. A normal race horse is admired and willing to give its all to feel successful. It is very competitive and image-conscious. A healthy hawk soars higher and higher. It is at ease, capable, alert and responds to the events of the moment. Its qualities are admirable.

TYPE 4 - THE ARTIST

DYSFUNCTIONAL	NORMAL	HEALTHY
Abandoned Cat	Mink	Black Panther

The dysfunctional abandoned cat feels alone and not wanted. It is sensitive, vulnerable, weak and shy. It feels sorry for itself and can be self-destructive. It secretly longs to be loved and accepted. It can be stormy and dangerous if not dealt with carefully. The normal mink is rare and unique. It feels good when it focuses on its uniqueness. However, it feels threatened and depressed when it feels that other people can see defects beneath its extraordinary fur. The healthy black panther is strong, calm, powerful, beautiful and mysterious. It is deeply self-aware.

TYPE 5 -THE THINKER

DYSFUNCTIONAL	NORMAL	HEALTHY
Fox	Badger	Owl

The dysfunctional fox is isolated, tricky, sneaky and self-serving. The normal badger is fiercely independent and is not interested in forming relationships with people. It is curious and investigates in detail whatever it encounters. The healthy owl is extremely perceptive and watchful. It is calmly aware of its inner self as well as the exterior world. It is an expert, open to seeing all and yet selective about what it pursues. When it chooses to or desires to it can readily interact with others.

TYPE 6 - THE LOYAL-SKEPTIC

DYSFUNCTIONAL	NORMAL	HEALTHY
Rabbit	Deer	German Shepherd

The dysfunctional rabbit is anxious, shy and over-reacts to expectations of danger. Its fearfulness is visible in its eyes. The normal deer is always alert to the possibility that danger will appear at any moment. It cooperates with other deer and obeys the commands of its leader. The healthy German shepherd is protective, reliable and loyal. It is on guard yet relaxed.

TYPE 7 - THE OPTIMIST

DYSFUNCTIONAL	NORMAL	HEALTHY
Mouse	Hummingbird	Butterfly

The dysfunctional mouse may be anxious, scattered and scurry around frantically, or it may be addicted to its search for cheese (fun). It is likely to panic and bite when its activities are interfered with. The normal hummingbird is either flying or resting. It wishes it could always fly around seeking the next sweet experience. The healthy butterfly is peaceful, relaxed and graceful as it explores the universe. It is joyous and accomplishes its many activities well.

TYPE 8 - THE CONTROLLER

DYSFUNCTIONAL	NORMAL	HEALTHY
Rhinoceros	Grizzly Bear	Tiger

The dysfunctional rhinoceros is powerful, dangerous and unpredictable. It will attack anything that moves. It has grandiose ideas about its capacities. The normal grizzly bear feels that it can do whatever it wants to do. It is powerful, intimidating and cunning. When it is provoked, it attacks ferociously. The healthy tiger is strong, alert and nobody messes with it. It is powerful and treated with respect.

TYPE 9 - THE PEACEMAKER

DYSFUNCTIONAL	NORMAL	HEALTHY
Turtle	Work Horse	Porpoise

The dysfunctional turtle is sluggish and lazy. At the first sign of conflict it withdraws into its shell. It doesn't care about much of anything except staying peacefully in its shell. The normal work horse trudges through life working hard and being responsible. It can't wait to get back to the barn to eat, sleep and relax. It isn't thrilled with the concept of work, but it is stuck in a rut and feels obliged to do what others want it to do. The healthy porpoise is in contact with its inner will and is loving, energetic, free flowing and at ease.

BIBLIOGRAPHY

BOOKS ABOUT THE ENNEAGRAM

Beesing, M., Robert J. Nogosek, and Patrick O'Leary. *The Enneagram: A Journey of Self-Discovery*. Denville, New Jersey: Dimension Books, 1984.

Hurley, Kathleen V., and Theodore E. Dobson. *What's My Type?*. San Francisco, Ca.: Harper San Francisco, 1992.

Keyes, Margaret F. *Emotions and the Enneagram: Working Through Your   Shadow Life Script*. Muir Beach, Ca.: Molysdatur, 1990.
_____ . *The Enneagram Relationship Workbook*. Muir Beach, Ca.: Molysdatur, 1992.

Naranjo, Claudio. *Ennea-Type Structures: Self-Analysis for the Seeker*. Nevada City, Ca.: Gateways, 1990.

Palmer, Helen. *The Enneagram: Understanding Yourself and Others in Your Life*. San Francisco: Harper and Row, 1988.

Riso, Don R. *Personality Types: Using the Enneagram for Self-Discovery*. Boston: Houghton Mifflin, 1987.
_____ . *Understanding the Enneagram: The Practical Guide to Personality Types*. Boston: Houghton Mifflin, 1990.

SELECTIVE GENERAL BIBLIOGRAPHY

American Psychiatric Association. *Diagnostic and Statistical Manual of Mental Disorders* (3rd ed., rev.) Washington, D.C.: American Psychiatric Association, 1987.

Almaas, A.H. *Essence.*York Beach: Samual Weisen, 1986.
_____ . *The Pearl Beyond Price*. Berkeley: Diamond Books, 1988.
_____ . *The Freedom to Be*. Berkeley: Diamond Books, 1989

Amodeo, John and Kris. *Being Intimate*. London: Arkana, 1986.

Bradshaw, John. *Home Coming*. New York: Bantam Books, 1990.

Dürekheim, Karlfried. *Hara, The Vital Centre of Man*, London: Unwin Hyman Limited, 1962.

Ellis, Albert, and Wendy Dryden. *The Practice of Rational Emotive Therapy* New York: Springer, 1987.

Fairbairn, W. and D. Ronald. *Psychodynamic Studies of the Personality,* London, Henley and Boston, 1984.

Fadiman, James, and Robert Frager. *Personality and Personal Growth*. New York, Harper and Row, 1976.

Freud, Sigmund. *The Basic Writings of Sigmund Freud*. New York: Random House, 1938.

Guntrip, Harry. *Psychoanalytic Theory, Therapy and the Self.* New York: Basic Books, 1973.

Gurdjieff, George I. *Views from the Real World*. New York: E.P. Dutton, 1973.

Halsey, A.H., ed. *Heredity and Environment*. New York: The Free Press, 1973.

Greenberg, Jay R., and Stephen A. Mitchell. *Object Relations in Psychoanalytic Theory.* Cambridge: Harvard University Press, 1983.

Horney, Karen. *Self-Analysis*. New York: W. W. Norton, 1942.

Jampossky, Gerald. *Love is Letting go of Fear*. Berkeley: Celestial Arts, 1979.

Mahler, Margaret S. et al. *The Psychological Birth of the Human Infant*. New York: International University Press, 1975.

Maslow, Abraham H. *Toward a Psychology of Being*. New York, D. Van Nostrand , 1968.
_____ . *Motivation and Personality*. Second Edition, New York, Harper and Row, 1970.

Miller, Alice. *Prisoners of Childhood*. New York: Basic Books, 1981.

Naranjo, Claudio. *How To Be*. Los Angeles: Tarcher, 1989.

Oldham, John M., and Lois Morris, *Personality Self-Portrait,* New York: Bantam Books, 1990.

Ouspensky, P. D. *The Fourth Way*. New York: Random House, 1971.

Perls, Fritz. *In and Out of the Garbage Pail*. Moab, UT: Real People Press, 1969.

Rajneesh, Bagwan Shree. *Only One Shy*. New York, E.P. Dutton, 1975.

Rosenberg, Jack, and Marjorie Rand. *Body, Self, and Soul- Sustaining Integration*. Atlanta: Humanics, 1985.

Schutz, Will. *The Truth Option*. Berkeley: Ten Speed Press, 1984.

Speeth, Kathleen R. *The Gurdjieff Work*. Los Angeles: Tarcher, 1989,

Wilson, Colin. *New Pathways in Psychology; Maslow and the Post-Freudian Revolution*. New York: New American Library, 1974.

GLOSSARY

Basic Trust - Basic trust is confidence that the universe is basically compassionate, supportive and intelligent.

Compelling Desire - Your compelling desire is the central, unconscious driving force underlying your personality, and it represents your primary hope for love and happiness.

Depth Psychology - Depth Psychology is an area of psychology which attributes your personality development primarily to conflicts and injuries which occurred early in your childhood and which are buried in your unconscious. Psychological growth happens as you become aware of these unconscious conflicts and injuries.

Essence - Essence is your nature, that which is most true, precious and real in you. It is that which existed at your birth but was buried under the fixated shell of your personality early in childhood. Most aspects of essence, such as love, strength and joy, are universal. One aspect of essence, personal essence, is unique to you. The degree to which your personal essence is developed, combined with the degree to which the various aspects of universal essence are readily available to you, determines your level of development and health.

Fixated Personality Shell - Your Fixated Personality Shell is comprised of the aspects of your personality which have been fixated since early childhood and form a shell around your essence. Your shell defends you from painful inner feelings, acts as a filter between you and reality, and blocks the emergence of your essence. It represents the incomplete development of your personal potential. Transpersonal psychologists often call the fixated personality shell the ego. According to William James, over ninety-nine percent of our personality is habitual (fixated).

Identification - Identification occurs when you take a small part of yourself to be your whole-self and cling to this identity. For example, you may identify with your body, saying to yourself, "I am my body," or you may identify with your mind saying, "I am my mind." You may be identified with power like a Type Eight or with love like a Type Two. When you identify with a small aspect of yourself you are not in touch with the larger reality of who you are.

Motivation - Motivation is anything which you learned while growing up which causes you to take action.

Personal Potential - Your personal potential is unlimited. It is well developed when the unique capacities of each Enneagram personality type, essence in general and your personal aspect of essence are readily available to you. They assume their natural place in the totality of your being. This allows you to respond to situations as they are, not as you want them to be or hope they are. The aspects of your personality and essence needed to respond to any situation arise spontaneously and effortlessly. You become balanced, at ease, fluid and flexible and able to interact creatively with your inner-self and the outer world.

Personality - Your personality is your tendency to think, feel and behave in a consistent manner over a long period of time and across a wide variety of situations. It is the familiar everyday self which you usually perceive yourself to be. It was established early in childhood and determines the way you relate to other people and the world now as an adult. Most of it is comprised of your fixated personality shell. Your personality is generally what transpersonal teachers refer to as the ego.

Psychodynamics - The psychology of mental and emotional processes established early in childhood which act primarily at an unconscious level.

Personality Type - One of the nine principal Enneagram personalities motivated primarily by a single underlying compelling desire.

Relaxation - A release of bodily tension which causes movement to a specific point on the Enneagram from another specific point on the Enneagram. For example, the Artists move to the Perfectionist Point when relaxed and seek greater perfection in whatever they do.

Stress - An increase in bodily and mental tension which causes movement to a specific point on the Enneagram from another specific point on the Enneagram. For example, the Artists move to the Pleaser's Point when stressed and become more helpful and compassionate.

Sub-types - Each personality type can be subdivided into three sub-types which have specific personality characteristics. These sub-types focus on the issues of self-preservation, social relationships and intimate relationships.

Transformation - Transformation involves a shift from seeking to gratify the fixated desires of your personality to discovering, and expressing the truth, love and joy of your essence. Transformation occurs as you relax and identify less with your personality and more with your essence.

Wings - Your Wings are the personality types on both sides of your type on the Enneagram. For example, the Wings for a Type Three personality are Types Two and Four.